PROMOTING POSITIVE PARENTING

Promoting Positive Parenting

A professional guide to establishing
groupwork programmes for parents of
children with behavioural problems

David Neville
Dick Beak
Liz King

arena

Published by
Arena
Ashgate Publishing Limited
Gower House
Croft Road
Aldershot
Hants GU11 3HR
England

Ashgate Publishing Company
Old Post Road
Brookfield
Vermont 05036
USA

British Library Cataloguing in Publication Data

Neville, David
    Promoting Positive Parenting
    I. Title
    362.828

ISBN 1 85742 266 X

Library of Congress Catalog Card Number: 95-77175

Typeset in Palatino by Manton Typesetters, 5–7 Eastfield Road, Louth, Lincolnshire LN11 7AJ.
Printed and bound in Great Britain by Biddles Ltd, Guildford.

Contents

Foreword

Sue Townsend

I am delighted to write the foreword for *Promoting Positive Parenting* which is about the work of the Centre for Fun and Families. I agreed to become the Patron for the Centre because I thought that a new approach was needed to help families cope with their difficulties. I have become increasingly concerned about the lack of support for parents who, out of desperation, are driven to slapping, smacking and shouting as ways of trying to control their children's behaviour. More often than not, alternative guidance is not available, leaving parents feeling helpless and alone.

In the long term, physical punishment does not work with children. It demeans both the child and the parents. A range of other methods are needed. The Centre's fun and families groupwork programme is able to help parents find a positive alternative! Sometimes it is a matter of education; one mother I knew expected her year-old daughter to be able to control her bowels and smacked her when she failed to 'perform' in her potty. Another parent flew into a rage because her two-year-old refused to eat everything set in front of him.

I have four children and now, happily, three small grandchildren. I have had many difficulties with my children over the years. I have made silly mistakes and at times been in despair, so I do know how very difficult it is to be a parent. I also know the joy that children can bring to parents. The Centre for Fun and Families wants to rekindle that joy and this book offers a practical guide for anyone working with children and families to run similar fun and families groups.

These are hard times for families, in the constant struggle to make ends meet, to find decent housing and somewhere safe for children to play. It is easy to forget that our children need something that costs us nothing: our time, patience and love. The fun and families programme can help parents to find these resources within themselves and feel proud of their achievements.

It is my hope that this book will be an invaluable guide to professional staff who work with parents to try a new and very positive approach to help them with the hardest but most rewarding job in the world – being a 'positive parent'.

Sue Townsend

Acknowledgements

The co-editors would like to thank the following people who have contributed to the development of the fun and families programme, the work of the Centre and have therefore made this book possible:

- Health visitors from Lutterworth and Broughton Astley with whom the fun and families groups were first piloted.
- Andy Gill, a co-founder of the Centre who pioneered with Dick Beak the first fun and families groups and shared in all the developments and work of the Centre until November 1993. His Ph.D research, work on evaluation, love of 'high-tech' gadgets, his enthusiasm, sense of humour and his continued support are all greatly valued.
- All the social work students who have been on placement at the Centre (23 at the time of writing), and have contributed so much in terms of new ideas and developments.
- All the professional workers from a variety of agencies with whom we have run groups, for their enthusiasm and support.
- All the members of our governing body who have supported us both through their encouragement and fundraising.
- Our Patron, Sue Townsend, for her support and to Martin Herbert, our Honorary Consultant for his help, advice and encouragement.
- Last, but not least, our partners and friends who have put up with us while we wrote and rewrote and then changed our minds, and then rewrote this book.

Introduction

Professor Martin Herbert

It seems very fitting to me to write the Introduction to this book since I have been involved in several ways in the origins, development and the theoretical approaches used by the Centre in the fun and families groupwork programme. For example, I was involved in supervising Andy Gill's research project, was able to offer the three co-founders advice on their plan to form a viable voluntary organisation and have been the Centre's Honorary Consultant since its formation in 1990.

In the light of my involvement and my knowledge of the co-founder's early hopes and ambitions for the groupwork programme, I am extremely pleased to see the progress they have been able to achieve, the evidence for which is amply demonstrated in the pages of this book. I feel this book is an important landmark in relation to work with children and families for a variety of reasons.

The theoretical foundation, social learning theory, upon which the fun and families groupwork programme is based, is now a thoroughly researched, well-proven and effective method of achieving change in behaviour. The workers at the Centre have succeeded in the remarkable objective of devising ways to make the theoretical model accessible to a wide range of parents in a simple and understandable form. At the same time they have made it fun!

The evaluations of the groupwork programme show that a preventative service can be effective and does not, if parents are empowered by the programme, run the risk of parents becoming dependent upon the service offered. This runs counter to some of the popular thinking that intervention with families should only occur at the point of crisis.

Of further importance is the fact that the fun and families groupwork programme is popular with parents, empowers parents and they feel that the service meets their needs. Consequently the programme is highly complementary to the duties that local authorities have under the Children Act (1989) to offer support to families and to work in partnership with them.

At the same time the programme is capable of being made relevant and accessible to parents of all races, culture, gender or disability and this book gives a central place to the theoretical and practical ways in which this can be achieved.

There is also great emphasis in the programme on ways in which co-working with other agencies can be successful. The programme is highly relevant to workers in social services departments, the health service, education and voluntary agencies. This is a very positive benefit at a time when inter-agency co-operation is at a premium in child protection work and family support.

Finally, this programme is able to meet the requirements of the 'buzz' words of the current decade. The fun and families programme is both economical, efficient and effective.

It seems to me that there are no valid arguments for not running fun and families groups. This is because not to do so is to reject a method of working that is based upon well-researched theory, is proven to improve child behaviours, empowers parents and encourages partnership, is anti-discriminatory, assists inter-agency co-operation and is efficient, effective and economical.

The co-editors of this book are all qualified social workers who have wide and long experience in work with children and families. They also have an enthusiasm for the fun and families group programme which they want to share with you. Consequently they have written this book in such a way that it can offer you a practical step-by-step guide to take you through the fun and families groupwork programme, and also a thorough introduction to the theoretical ideas that underpin the programme's structure and method. I very much welcome its publication and am sure it will be widely read and very thoroughly used.

Part I

The background and history of the Centre for Fun and Families

1 The development of the Centre

This book is intended to give you a guide to all aspects of the theoretical approaches and the practical details of the fun and families groupwork programme. The theoretical basis of our work includes social learning theory, groupwork skills and cognitive behavioural theory applied with attention to empowerment and anti-discriminatory practice. These practical details will include how to plan the group, the groupwork skills required to run it, the content of the weekly session, how to evaluate the work and how to develop ongoing support for parents when the group ends. All these matters are considered in the context of anti-discriminatory practice. Finally, the last chapter will look at future directions the Centre hopes to take and gives you information on how to seek help if things do not go to plan and how to get in touch with us to tell us when it has all gone very well! We publish a national newsletter and try to publicise all the good work that is being undertaken throughout the country approximately four times a year.

Defining the terms used in the book

This book, *Promoting Positive Parenting*, has been written to give people who work with families and children a guide to the group programme called 'fun and families groups'. This has been developed by the staff of the Centre for Fun and Families. It is important, at the start of this guide, to offer a few definitions of the terms used throughout the book so that you can proceed with a common understanding of the language employed. The most important terms you will come across are 'fun and families groups', 'social learning theory' and the 'Centre for Fun and Families'. We will start with a brief description of each of these terms.

What is a 'fun and families group'?

A fun and families group is a seven-week intensive parent training programme designed to help parents whose children are displaying behaviour difficulties such as aggression, defiance, temper tantrums or sleep problems. The main objective of the group is to apply social learning theory or behavioural principles to individual child-care circumstances. It is designed to help parents make clear sense of what their children are doing and why. It is intended to give practical, down-to-earth suggestions to assist them to change their children's behaviour and to allow them to regain parenthood as a 'fun' experience.

What is social learning theory?

The basic assumption of social learning theory is that social behaviour is learned and can be changed by altering the way parents respond to and manage their child's behaviour. In simple terms, if parents want to encourage good behaviour they should positively reinforce or reward it, and if they want to reduce unwanted behaviour they should discourage it through a range of methods referred to as 'punishment'. These methods include ignoring, withdrawal of privileges, time out, etc., all of which have been shown to be more effective than physical punishments. A range of other means of assisting children to learn acceptable social behaviours include modelling, prompting and giving clear instructions.

What is the Centre for Fun and Families?

The Centre for Fun and Families is a national voluntary organisation with charitable status (Charity no. 328640), which was established in 1990. The Centre is based in Leicester (25 Shanklin Drive, Knighton, Leicester LE2 3RH, phone 0116 270 7198). The objective of the Centre is to support parents, who are experiencing behaviour and communication difficulties with their children, through the development and promotion of effective groupwork programmes. The Centre offers programmes for parents with young children and parents with teenage children. The programme for parents with younger children is called 'Fun and Families', and the programme for parents with teenage children is called 'Living with Teenagers'.

Within Leicestershire the Centre runs a regular programme of groups for parents in partnership with other agencies such as health visitors, schools and voluntary organisations. Outside Leicestershire the Centre provides training and consultancy services to both statutory and voluntary agencies throughout the country on the setting-up and running of these groupwork programmes. To support these programmes the Centre has produced a range of resources, including nine booklets, a video, a relaxation tape for parents and sets of fun stickers and albums. The Centre also offers student placements for students on Diploma in Social Work courses to allow them to experience the planning and running of a fun and families group.

The Centre is committed to providing services to people of any race, sex, religion, disability and sexual orientation, and has an anti-discriminatory practice policy and action plan.

Information on the details of resources and services available from the Centre are given at the end of this book.

The history of the development of the Centre

It can be imagined that the development of a major group programme and the formation of a new voluntary organisation did not occur rapidly or by chance. The ideas came together gradually, piece by piece, between 1987 and 1990 as a result of the convergence of a number of developments.

Development of the group programme

In 1987 a number of social services staff in south Leicestershire were interested in two themes. First, the application of methods derived from social learning theory was thought to be practical and effective in work with families with child behaviour difficulties. Second, there was an interest in a community social work approach to empowering clients to use their own resources and of seeking out resources in the community, for instance other agencies, who may have a common interest in helping families.

In terms of the help available to families, health visitors featured prominently. Even before groupwork projects were devised, liaison with health visitors had developed so that meetings and shared workshops were a regular feature. The time spent getting to know, understand and establish a common theoretical base was very significant. Once these simple behavioural ideas were put into practice with parents, a reputation was created in the community that there were practitioners available who could actually help. Equally important, the advice was not overly intrusive and was seen to be effective. The result of this was that more referrals were generated than either the social services staff or health visitors could cope with.

Therefore, in 1987 the first discussions began about setting up groups which could cater for families experiencing difficulty in managing their children's behaviour. Drawing on research and experience, an eight-week programme (later refined to seven weeks) was devised during which parents could learn about and practice techniques with a proven track record in changing child behaviours.

However good a programme is, it would have a limited impact unless it was presented in an attractive fashion. Those involved took great pains to offer potential referral sources such as doctors and schools with the programme details and research references so that a high level of credibility was established. Additionally, efforts were made to attract potential clients. An attractive invitation was sent rather than a letter. The first session was to be a social one, with wine and food provided, and offering the opportunity for participants to comment on the proposed programme and suggest additions or changes if they felt it was necessary.

The name for the group was also agonised over and there was a wish to have an attractive title that made the objectives of the group clear. It was recognised that most participants had largely lost the sense of how much fun parents can obtain from bringing up children and were caught in a downward spiral of recrimination, frustration and helplessness. Consequently the label 'fun and families groups' was chosen to reflect the group's serious objective of helping families to recapture the lost sense of the fun in bringing up their children.

This aim was pursued with enthusiasm and parents in the early groups taught us a great deal and helped to shape subsequent programmes. Each parent is the only real expert so far as their own child is concerned and it was quickly made evident that more time had to be allocated to considering individual circumstances and allowing informal discussion (providing it was guided to keep on task) between parents. The encouragement the parents drew from each other was also noted as a major feature of the group's effectiveness. Gradually, through the feedback from group evaluations, the programme was refined to a seven-week programme in which the minimum necessary theoretical ideas can be presented and the parents' own strengths can be brought to bear on choosing the best way to achieve positive change for the whole family.

The development of the Centre

Developing an effective group programme that empowers parents in partnership with another agency, while working within a busy social services department, is a major challenge in itself. Taking this further to develop a completely new voluntary organisation was an even greater challenge and required an even more unique set of circumstances to prevail. Important factors in encouraging the development of the concept of the Centre are discussed below.

By 1989, the fun and families group programme had been refined and improved to the point that it had become locally known to parents as an effective and popular group programme to join. In addition, the parent support groups, made up of parents who had experienced the programme had felt that similar groups should be set up in other parts of the country. Consequently they wrote several articles in the local press. Furthermore, Andy Gill, one of the co-founders, wrote an article in the social work press (1989b). The result of all this publicity was that Dick Beak, Andy Gill and the health visitors who had been running the groups began to receive requests for information from agencies all over the country. It rapidly became obvious that the concept of fun and families groups was one that people wanted to know about and a variety of agencies were interested in running similar groups. The problem for those involved was how to respond to this while working full time in a statutory setting.

Within the social services department that employed the Centre's co-founders there were two ominous forces at work. First, a further re-organisation was pending which meant that much developmental work was in danger of being put on hold. Second, the effects of successive Government cut-backs and local policy changes were leading to a situation in which any work with families, other than child protection work, would be impossible to sustain. On the positive side, there was a growing confidence that voluntary organisations would be funded by social services departments, in line with guidance given in the Children Act (1989).

The combination of the above two factors led the co-founders to test the viability of launching a voluntary organisation by producing a questionnaire to all social services departments and members of the Behavioural Social Work Group. They were more than surprised to find that the response was more than double the expected response for a postal questionnaire, and the replies were all very positive. Taking the idea further, the co-founders held a national conference in Leicester in February 1990. The conference was over-subscribed, attracting over 80 people, including almost 20 parents. From these efforts to test demand it was obvious that there was a tremendous interest in the services the Centre hoped to offer.

Another factor that was of considerable importance was that the three co-founders had worked together since 1987. While all three had different interests and styles of working they recognised the value of each other's contribution to the concept of the Centre. Consequently, very good working relationships had developed which were going to be essential in guiding a new organisation through the uncharted waters that lay ahead.

Having established, in principle, that the formation of a voluntary organisation was viable the co-founders needed to find the last piece of the jigsaw puzzle: how to fund the organisation? They knew that any new organisation would have high initial set-up costs because of the need to acquire equipment and to publicise and promote the organisation. In addition, the services the Centre intended to provide, such as training and consultancy, could not be relied upon to give a regular, consistent source of income. After considerable searching and discussion it was decided that each co-founder would seek some part-time employment that would give a regular source of income. By March 1990 Dick Beak and David Neville had been accepted to do guardian *ad litem* work on the Leicestershire Panel of Guardians and Andy Gill was still searching for a part-time post. The decision was taken to launch the Centre on 1 June 1990, with Dick and David starting in June and Andy joining slightly later in November 1990.

The development and growth of the Centre

In the five years of the Centre's development, from June 1990 to June 1995, there has been very rapid growth and development in the services and resources on offer. The main growth in the Centre's services have occurred in the following areas.

Workshops

The Centre originally commenced its training work with one workshop about 'Setting up and running a fun and families group'. The Centre now has six workshop packages on offer. The other main Workshop is on the 'Living with Teenagers' programme. The others are on related subjects such as 'Empowerment' , 'Written Agreements', 'Promoting Positive Parenting' and 'Promoting Positive Parenting for Foster Carers and Adopters'. Our initial training/consultancy was done in Leicestershire but over four years we have been involved as widely as County Durham, North Yorkshire, Bradford, Rotherham, Lancashire, St. Helen's, Trafford, Stockport Wirral, Wolverhampton, Walsall, Solihull, Warwickshire, Lincolnshire, Essex, Gloucestershire, Somerset, South and Mid Glamorgan and Guernsey.

Student placement

The Centre had no initial plans to offer student placements but the popularity of the placement has led to 20 students to date being offered the opportunity to run groups. The Centre now regularly offers 6 placements per year.

Resources

The Centre commenced life with only one booklet on offer. Due to the repeated requests for literature to support the training, eight additional booklets have been written, details of which are given at the end of this book. The writing of this book is, of course, another major landmark for the Centre. In addition to the booklets, a video with associated practice manual has been produced by Andy Gill in partnership with the Rugby Family

Centre. A relaxation tape for parents has also been produced. A particularly pleasing resource are the fun stickers, guidance leaflet and sticker albums which are used in fun and families groups to encourage children's good behaviour. The stickers and album were designed by a parent who had attended a fun and families group run by Andy Gill at the Rugby Family Centre.

Spread of groups

The fun and families groups in Leicestershire were originally only run in Lutterworth and Broughton Astley. However, they have now spread to Hinckley, Market Harborough, Melton Mowbray and into the Highfields, Belgrave and St Matthew's areas of the city of Leicester.

Multi-cultural expansion

The groups were originally only run for white parents but groups for Asian parents have been developed. This has led the Centre to produce resources for groupwork in Gujarati and to make a range of partnerships with staff in the Asian community. This work has been in parallel to the Centre's development of an anti-discriminatory practice policy and action plan.

The Centre started with three white, male staff. With Andy Gill's departure to work as Project Leader, NSPCC (Portsmouth) in November 1993, the opportunity was taken to remedy the lack of black or female staff. Consequently, Liz King joined the staff in November 1993.

Fundraising and information distribution

The Centre had an original governing body of three people who applied for charitable status and drew up the Centre's constitution. The governing body now consists of eight people and there is now a permanent fundraising sub-committee. This sub-committee takes on the role of applying to grant-making trusts and businesses for funds throughout the year and has doubled the grant income of the Centre since it was formed.

Finally, the information about the Centre is much more available and professionally organised. There is now a workshop programme, resources catalogue, student placements booklet and several information booklets for parents.

We hope that this chapter has given you an introduction to the history, formation, growth and development of the Centre, its fun and families programme and the social learning theory on which it is based.

2 Planning a fun and families group

First thoughts

The most essential points to bear in mind when thinking about running a fun and families group are:

- The most important resource you have is your own skills, experience and local knowledge.
- Each group will be different in some ways so be prepared to be flexible and make changes if problems arise.
- Try and make sure you give yourself enough time to plan before the group starts and before each session.

You will need to draw on your skills, experience and local knowledge and to feel confident that you can make good use of these. We stress this because we are aware that some fun and families groups have been run in a wide variety of settings, with parents of varying affluence, from different racial and cultural groups and with different proportions of male and female parents. Our experience has been that the group programme seems to be equally effective in most settings but difficulties have most frequently occurred where staff we have trained to run groups have not given sufficient attention to adapting the programme to local circumstances.

Consequently we would urge you to draw on your own skills and knowledge to tackle the issues of racism, sexism and any other forms of discrimination and your sense of the concerns of your local community, because they are the essential ingredients for running a group on your patch. Examples of the relevance of such knowledge are given throughout this book.

The majority of the material in the rest of this chapter has been derived from discussions and contributions made at conferences and workshops held in parts of the country as far apart as Guernsey, Wolverhampton, Essex, Wirral, South Glamorgan, North Yorkshire or Seaham near Sunderland. The material can serve as a checklist of matters that need to be attended to in the successful planning of a group. The important task for you is to undertake the planning of these matters while bearing in mind the nature and context of the environment in which you are working.

A planning checklist

It is useful to have an initial checklist of all the items that require thought before the group starts. From our experience most workers who are running a fun and families group for the first time need about two months to make sure all these matters have been dealt with. However, workers running subsequent groups can often complete the planning process in four to six weeks. In the rest of this chapter we will list all the issues that usually need to be considered and give some thought on how plans can be made to resolve them. There are some issues relating to race, gender and disability that require more detailed planning and we will deal with these issues in the second section of this chapter.

Size of group

Experience suggests that a group size of about eight to ten people is ideal. This is most likely to consist of perhaps one or two couples and four to six individuals. If the group is bigger, individuals, particularly the least able or vocal, tend to get lost and their concerns are not fully addressed. If the group is smaller the group tends to lack the range of experience and tends to become more prone to domination by one or two individuals. Also, if, in small groups of, for example, less than six, one or two people don't attend, the group is in danger of folding up. We have recently had some experience of running groups for 12–15 people. This can work but it has required the use of three co-leaders. In addition, it has been noticeable that while the overall evaluation for the group has been just as good as smaller groups, there is a tendency for people who are less able, due to lack of literacy skills or intellectual difficulties, to do less well in larger groups.

Composition of the group

There are several matters that need to be considered in terms of group composition. These include race, gender, age of children and the nature of the behaviours that the parent is concerned about. The issues of race and gender will be dealt with in section two of this chapter.

In terms of the age of the children, experience has suggested that running groups for parents with children of widely varying ages is difficult and probably less effective. Groups for parents of children aged two to twelve years can be effective but it is helpful to have at least two parents with children aged over five years. Otherwise, a lone parent with a child over five years may have no basis for comparison or support, bearing in mind that the fun and families programme makes very good use of the support and advice available from parents within the group.

We have found that parents of teenagers need to focus on similar social learning theory principles but skills in listening, communication, problem solving and negotiation become much more important. Consequently, the Centre has begun to pilot a separate groupwork programme for parents of teenagers called 'Living with teenagers – a family survival programme'. Details of this programme are available from the Centre.

There does seem to be an advantage, if possible, to running a group with parents who are experiencing different degrees of severity of behaviour difficulty. For example, running a group solely for parents who have abused their children can pose major difficulties. Such a group may have greater initial negativity and helplessness which may inhibit progress. There may also be greater worries about stigma from parents, especially if their attendance has any degree of coercion or compulsion about it. Our experience has been that a mix of parents, some of whom have their children's names on the child protection register and some who are experiencing less severe difficulties, is most productive. Such a mix can best be achieved by allowing referrals from a range of sources, including self-referrals. Your local knowledge of other agencies and their readiness to refer is important here. Generally, health visitors have access to a wide range of potential referrals.

Where to run a group

Generally speaking, groups seem to be most successful when they are run in premises that are neutral or non-threatening. Community centres, or other types of facility that do not stigmatise participants are useful. Social services offices, schools or other premises associated with formal agencies can be extremely off-putting to parents. However, local knowledge is again vital when planning for your venue because some premises can be a lot more welcoming than others. For example, we recently ran a group in a school because it had good facilities, including a kitchen and crèche, and also because one of the parents took part in the planning process and persuaded the other parents to come. The parent also made very good cakes! Also, if you are attempting to attract people from different racial and cultural backgrounds you need to be sensitive to the significance for the parents of the location you choose.

Some locations also have other advantages. Family centres often can provide child-care facilities for parents which can be a great asset. In rural areas, where transport can be a major obstacle, a location offering access to public transport can be useful.

When to run a group

There are varying advantages according to whether you plan to run a group in the evening or during the working day. The advantages of evening groups seem to be:

- It is possible to attract men to such groups although, in itself, it does not guarantee their attendance.
- It seems possible to develop the informal, social element of the group more effectively.
- Other work pressures are less likely to interfere with the running of the group, assuming you have the energy left at the end of a draining day to run a group!

The advantages of day time groups appear to be:

- You can do it in work time!
- Child-care and transport facilities are easier to arrange.
- Other professional staff may be happier to work with you during the day.

From the experience of trying a range of different times, the most consistently successful seems to be between 9.30/10am to 11.30am/12pm. The afternoon presents problems because parents may need to pick up children from school.

Who to run a group with

A wide variety of professional staff becomes involved in work with children and their families. We are aware of a range of groups being run by social workers and health visitors, family centre staff and social workers, workers from voluntary agencies and educational psychologists and social workers and their colleagues from child guidance units. Such partnerships in running groups make great sense because, apart from the obvious advantage of sharing professional skills, time, experience and mutual support, it is possible to share:

- Premises and equipment, for example, video, flip charts or photo-copying facilities
- Transport
- Referral sources
- Costs of planning and running a group
- Publicity
- Child-care facilities
- Female or male workers or workers from a variety of races.

Another useful spin-off is that inter-agency relationships often improve very dramatically when a new, positive innovation in working practice is shared. This spin-off should not be underestimated. The improvement in working relationships and the consequent raising of morale can dramatically reduce the workload and cut down on frustrating and time-consuming wrangles that are often the bane of our lives in the caring professions.

The list below is a good prompt to help you use your local information to think of all the professional staff who might work with children and families who are experiencing behaviour difficulties:

- Health visitor
- Social worker
- NSPCC (local contact)
- Family centre
- Education welfare
- Child guidance
- Family service unit
- Homestart

Publicity – how to attract families

From the experience of running groups for over four years it is apparent that word-of-mouth recommendations of the effectiveness of the group-work are the best publicity medium. However, that is not a lot of help to you when you are planning your first group!

There are a number of options you can select. First, co-working with other agencies is very helpful since other professionals will be aware of families who might benefit from referral to a fun and families group. Second, it is helpful to use local publications, newspapers or community newspapers. Again, your local knowledge and contacts are vital here because you need to make sure that the local press will actually print what you want so that a positive image of the group can be fostered. Finally the use of leaflets and posters also works but you need to locate these where the parents you want to attract will see them. Health centres, doctor's surgeries, newsagents, libraries, community centres and schools can be good locations. Publicising the group through other professionals can also be a good idea.

Remember, in your publicity effort, that social services departments and other statutory agencies are a source of fear for many parents and their anxieties have been raised by the media. It is therefore essential to stress a positive and helpful image in your publicity material. This is not an approach that professionals are given a lot of opportunity to practice but the Centre has a range of examples of newspaper articles about fun and family groups that are available, upon request.

The place of evaluation in your group programme

There are many good reasons for planning to evaluate your groupwork with parents:

- Your managers will want to know how effective your groupwork is.
- It helps parents to see how much they have achieved.
- It helps you to assess whether some approaches work better than others.
- Finally, it is always good practice to evaluate what you do, and it conveys a sense of professionalism and care about quality to parents.

Basically, the evaluation can simply consist of establishing a 'baseline'. This is achieved by obtaining the parent's rating of their child's behaviour prior to the start of the group and comparing this with the parent's assessment when the group has finished. This can be done by using a child behaviour rating scale. There are many of these available. The Centre has produced its own and we also use the Eyberg Child Behaviour Inventory. Both of these can be obtained from the Centre. There is also one in Martin Herbert's *Working with Children and their Families* (Herbert, 1988, p. 17).

Contact with families before the group

Our experience would suggest that home visits prior to the group are *essential*, preferably by one or more of the group leaders. We would stress this because the failure to do home visits has been the most frequent cause of group failure, because hardly anyone turned up to the first session. The home visit serves a number of purposes:

- It ensures that the parents have met at least one group leader prior to the group's first session.

- It raises the parent's enthusiasm for the group and ensures that the parents have sorted out the potential problems of child care and transport which could prevent them arriving at the group.
- It enables the group leaders to check out that the group programme is the best way to offer help to that particular family.
- Potential difficulties such as literacy or disability can be noted and thereby dealt with tactfully during the group sessions.
- Any matters in relation to the family's race or culture, or a family member's gender or disability can be noted in order to make the group as relevant as possible to each individual parent.
- It gives the opportunity to commence the evaluation by asking the parents to complete a child behaviour inventory.
- Home visits give the opportunity to meet both parents and to try to persuade both parents to attend.

Transport, child care and refreshments

These very practical issues are clearly matters that rely on local knowledge and circumstances, but they can make all the difference to the effective running of the group so do not neglect them. We have been particularly struck by how the provision of crèche facilities can really help to persuade parents to keep coming along. For example, we recall how one child literally dragged his mother along to the group because he enjoyed the crèche so much. We also recall one Family Centre worker who said that for the first two sessions most of the parents admitted that they had only come to the group for a two-hour break from their children without much expectation that they would get anything else from it.

Refreshments are also an important part of creating a warm, welcoming atmosphere and help to establish the informal side of the group's task. This is very important when you bear in mind the considerable anxiety most parents feel when first attending a group. It is also important to make sure that you think about the right type of refreshments, especially if you are aware from your home visits that people with varying dietary requirements or habits are attending the group.

One group run by Family Centre staff recently had very poor attendance because transport was not offered. When feedback from those not attending was received it was clear that the prospect of getting several children ready to bring on public transport was just too much to cope with.

Obtaining commitment and funding from managers

While this may not be a planning problem for all workers, it is an important consideration that sometimes needs to be tackled. Otherwise, the lack of funding or commitment from managers can undermine all the other good work you have already done.

In order to assist in the process of convincing your managers that running fun and families groups is a good idea we have developed a list of arguments, based on the word 'changes':

Cost effective – helps ten families at once, uses parents as resources and can be run with others

Here and now – focus is on each parent's agenda and how change can be achieved within the seven weeks

Anxiety and stress reducing – parents regain control, and family and individual stress is reduced

Networks – informal support of parents develop and networking with other agencies grows

Growth of confidence – group programme empowers parents to tackle other issues in their lives

Evidence of effectiveness – evaluations demonstrate consistent reductions in poor child behaviour

Sharing of skills and resources with other agencies – creates good inter-agency relationships.

You may find it useful to add other items according to local circumstances while retaining the central arguments.

Funding is very much a matter of local budgeting practice but a few general points can be made:

- The major cost is staff time which is normally already paid for, so the additional costs tend to be for publicity, refreshments, hand-outs, booklets for parents and photocopying. Again, many of these are already available in larger statutory or voluntary agencies. A recent estimate done for an agency was that running a fun and families group would take roughly 32 hours over a four-month period to plan, do home visits and run the group. This would work out at between two and three hours per week.
- Two agencies working together can give you access to double the sources of funding.
- Where there are outstanding costs other than staff time the sources to meet these can include the following:

1) Preventive aid money can be used by social services departments on the grounds that children are being prevented from coming into care. If parents with children on the Child Protection Register attend the group, there is a very strong argument for the use of this type of funding.
2) Voluntary agencies can sometimes obtain seed money or small grants to start up new projects.
3) Many agencies have book budgets, play equipment or other budgets which can provide some of the resources needed.
4) Some agencies have reprographic departments which can produce leaflets or posters at low or no cost, providing your managers sanction it. However, they can take three to four weeks to produce so plan ahead!

- Charities or grant-making trusts are not an ideal source of funding but if you do have a good local contact they can often produce the small sums necessary for non-staff resources.

Race, gender, disability and sexual orientation

The Centre has a commitment to anti-discriminatory practice and great effort has been made to promote good practice in groupwork in such a way as to demonstrate that commitment. Before looking in detail at ways in which these issues can begin to be addressed in the planning of a group programme, it is worth looking at some of the basic assumptions of the fun and families group programme that can assist you in developing anti-discriminatory practice.

The most important point to stress is that in fun and families groups the parents are the key people in setting the agenda for change. There is no question, therefore, of telling parents which behaviours to alter or how to alter the behaviour. The purpose of the groups is to help parents define for themselves exactly *what* behaviour they want to change, to develop their own understanding of *why* that particular behaviour occurs and to select, from a range of options, *how* to change their child's behaviour.

In theory, at least, such an approach is not 'value laden' and should be accepting of the social, cultural and religious values of any parent. However, in practice every group leader carries their own personal and social biases in making judgements and it is important to be aware of these when planning your group programme.

When planning a group it is important to promote anti-discriminatory attitudes. In discussions in staff and student meetings we have concluded that the most effective way to do this is to include a discussion in the first session on the aims of the group; this permits the opportunity to outline briefly the Centre's commitment to avoiding any racist, sexist or discriminatory language. In addition it is important to ensure that your presentation and material offers positive images of black people, women, people with disabilities or gay people.

Race issues

The view of the Centre is that it is vital that groupwork approaches, as a means of offering help to parents experiencing behaviour difficulties with their children, should be available to people of all races. We are committed to offering this service and run groups in the Leicester area for Asian and African-Caribbean families, in co-operation with other statutory agencies such as health visitors and schools. In the rest of this section when we use the word 'black' we are using it as a short way of referring to any person who is not white.

The following ideas are derived from our experience, discussions that have taken place in workshops and our own anti-racist training.

Ideal strategies

It is preferable to start by looking for the best way to run a group that will attract people from all races, and then to consider other options that might be possible if optimum conditions do not exist.

Ideally, the way to run a group that will include people from different races is to ensure that the group leaders are representative of the races of the catchment area of the group. This will probably involve seeking out group leaders from the Asian or African-Caribbean communities. This approach is preferable because:

- The group leaders will have a good knowledge of the needs, wishes and aspirations of those communities. Such knowledge will greatly assist the process of communication and help in raising the enthusiasm for the group in those communities.
- Co-working with group leaders from different races will help to attain a presentation and choice of material that does not fall foul of the personal bias and prejudice that we all carry.
- The planning process will be assisted on such matters as where and when to run a group and how to publicise the group because of the workers' knowledge of their own community.
- When group leaders from different races work together, a clear and obvious statement is made about your agency's intentions to run anti-discriminatory services for a multi-racial community.

- Most importantly, our experience is that working with black staff is the most effective way of ensuring that you are successful in attracting and retaining black families to the group programme.

Other options

Due to the impact of institutional racism it may not be possible to locate black workers in your agency to help run a group. It is also not always possible for black workers to offer the required time since they may have other priorities that are equally demanding of their attention. We recognise that immense demands upon black colleagues may lead to us abusing them, because a scarcity of black workers can lead to an excessive workload. Finally, black workers may feel that they do not have the necessary skills or experience to co-run a group.

It is quite possible, however, to locate black workers who may be able to assist in other agencies. Local voluntary agencies may be able to help as well. Once again your local contacts and knowledge are invaluable in this search.

If, after an exhaustive search to find black workers, or to obtain their help, you are not successful, there are two other possible options:

- Seek the assistance of respected figures in the black community. Although they may not have the necessary skills or wish to act as group leaders, they will be able to make invaluable contributions to the group programme and give the work of the group greater credibility.
- Alternatively, seek the help of black parents who you may have worked with in another capacity, such as a volunteer or as a parent in a fun and families group. It would be particularly useful if they had some understanding of the nature of the groupwork programme.

Overall, it has to be said that these other options are second-best. Our experience is that they are much less likely to work. Also, we feel that our long-run objective should be to develop expertise in running fun and families groups amongst black workers, and this is going to be most rapidly achieved by working with black staff from the outset.

Gender issues

There seem to be two main areas concerning gender that need attention when planning a group:

- The need to persuade both parents to come to the group, thereby acknowledging that the care of their children is a joint responsibility.

- The need to address prevailing sexist attitudes in society through the inclusion of relevant material in the groupwork programme designed to promote non-sexist approaches to child care.

Parental attendance

Professional staff, when running groups, have had varying success in achieving the attendance of both parents or carers. Our groups have rarely managed to attain more than 25–30% male attendance. Consequently, it is not possible to offer any tried or tested formula for success. Daytime groups seem to have the lowest rate of success in attracting male partners. Despite this there are many daytime groups that do attract many men who either work shifts or are unemployed.

We are coming to the view that greater success will be achieved if a specific effort is made at the home visit stage to include both carers in the discussions. In particular, this is likely to be effective because it will help raise the enthusiasm of both partners and also help them to understand the importance of their attendance at the group. It will also help both parents to set to work on solving the problems of child-care arrangements, since one of the most common excuses for non-attendance given by male partners is that they have to stay at home to care for their children! Another important factor seems to be the co-working of both female and male group leaders so that men do not feel isolated or that they are attending a women's group.

There may be some circumstances in which workers may wish to plan deliberately for an all-female (or all-male) group. If this is the case, it would be worth spending time looking at the content of the programme and making necessary changes, since the programme has been structured on the assumption of a mix of male and female parents.

Promoting non-sexist attitudes

Group discussions with parents over seven sessions will almost inevitably raise some issues about prevailing sexist attitudes in society. However, if you are committed to non-sexist practice you will want to introduce some material at strategic points in the programme in order to make sure you do not have to rely on chance.

From discussions we have had on this subject there seem to be some good points in the programme to introduce ideas about the different ways that females and males are treated in families. For example, in the second session of the group, we begin by looking at the concept of what is 'normal' behaviour for children. This seems a good point to ask the group to look at whether they find some behaviour more acceptable for girls than for boys and how these attitudes might have arisen. In addition, in session five, where parents' thoughts and feelings and dealing with stress are considered, the need to share responsibilities and support each other can be raised.

It is also important to check and reflect on all the material you might use to make sure that it does not inadvertently reinforce sexist stereotypes. It is equally important to be prepared to challenge any sexist statements made in the group in such a way that makes clear your commitment to anti-discriminatory practice without offending or embarrassing the group member who made the statement.

Disability and sexual orientation

In terms of lessons learned the Centre has no direct experience of running groups for parents of children with disabilities or for gay people, although it is part of our anti-discriminatory policy action plan to do so as soon as possible. Consequently, it was not felt helpful to attempt to offer practical guidelines in this part of the book. However, Chapter 3 offers a theoretical framework that should assist in the planning of a group for parents of children with disabilities, or gay parents.

Clearly, the area of groupwork dealing with anti-discriminatory practice requires considerable skill and sensitivity and requires careful planning to achieve good practice. It is important, however, not to feel discouraged – you are more likely to run into problems due to inadequate planning than you are through trying to get it right and making a few mistakes. We have found that some staff and students can allow this area of work to become so anxiety-provoking and contentious that the eventual outcome is that nothing is achieved or attempted: this is the worst outcome of all.

Part II

The theoretical background

3 Empowerment and anti-discriminatory practice

During the development of the Centre and the fun and families group programme, the two themes of empowerment and anti-discriminatory practice have been central to our thinking and action. We will look at each of these concepts in turn and look at the theoretical background and practical implications of these for our fun and families group work programme. The practical application of these theoretical concepts to the fun and families programme is dealt with in detail in Part III.

Empowerment

We first offer a definition of empowerment, then consider the expected outcomes of empowering parents, look at the empowering aspects of the fun and families programme and finally look at the evidence that these outcomes occur for parents attending fun and families groups.

Definition of empowerment

The concepts of user involvement, participation, partnership and empowerment are all, to some degree, interchangeable and all present considerable difficulty in being precisely and acceptably defined. For the purposes of the work of the Centre we have used the definition offered by Beresford and Croft (1990): 'making it possible for people who are disempowered to exercise power and to have more control over their lives. This means having a greater voice in institutions, agencies and situations that effect them' (p. 47).

Expected outcomes of empowering parents

From a literature search on the anticipated outcomes of empowering parents, the following are thought to result from increasing the influence parents have on a service:

- Parents attain increased dignity and self-respect.
- Decision-making about individual services are based on the best, most accurate, information.
- Services are more appropriate to parents' needs.
- Parents' problem-solving skills are improved.
- Greater diversity and choice of services develop to meet parents' needs more appropriately.
- Forward planning of services is based upon the best information and therefore more accurately reflects clients' needs.

Empowering aspects of the fun and families group programme

Various aspects of the fun and families groupwork programme are instrumental in empowering parents who attend. First, parents are able to choose for themselves the behaviours they want to change and are also able to select for themselves the methods, from a range of alternatives, that they wish to use to achieve behaviour change. In addition, parents can offer and receive support from other parents. This is actively encouraged by group leaders, both in the programme and also in the design of the activities and exercises.

The approach of social learning theory does not apportion blame for behaviours but offers methods for change. It thus avoids parents feeling that they have 'failed' or are 'problem parents'. Social learning theory's approach removes the stigma or moral sting of failure and therefore improves parents' self-esteem. The language and methods used in the programme are down to earth, free of jargon and designed to be non-threatening and supportive.

There is an emphasis on not keeping any records of the group, except basic factual details such as name, address and phone number. The only other material that is kept relates to the evaluation of the group which is usually kept anonymously, in the form of Parent 1, Parent 2, etc. This makes parents feel that they are in control of the information they offer in the group.

It is also important that the parents are aware that the programme has been consistently evaluated to have a high success rate which builds parental confidence that positive change can be achieved. The step-by-step practical approach, plus the emphasis in the fifth session on offering positive challenges to negative thoughts and feelings, greatly enhances parents' feelings of confidence and self-esteem.

Finally, in the first session, there is a very strong emphasis on developing an encouraging, approachable and friendly group atmosphere. The aims of the group are clearly explained and parents are offered the opportunity to participate in setting out their expectations of what should happen in the group.

Do fun and families groups empower parents and are the expected outcomes achieved?

An important question that has been raised throughout the development of the fun and families programme has been whether the programme succeeds in achieving the outcomes expected from the process of empowering parents. The Centre was greatly assisted in trying to answer this question by Andy Gill (the Centre's co-founder) in his Ph.D research project which looked at the key elements of the fun and families group programme that made it effective for parents. It is useful to look in turn at each of the expected outcomes of empowering parents and at the evidence for the assertion that fun and families groups do succeed in empowering parents.

Increased dignity and self-respect

It is clear from the comments parents have made on the research questionnaires that they feel much better about themselves and what they have achieved by the end of a fun and families group. Comments on this subject have included:

- 'We are all proud of what we have achieved and feel we cared enough to change the situation.'
- 'Before attending the course I felt totally helpless and alone. Being able to share difficulties and get practical advice that works has helped me to be less confused and more confident about the future.'
- 'I can see now that my difficulties are not as unusual or bad as I thought. This helps.'

Decision making about individual services are based upon the best, most accurate information

Decisions about which behaviour to change and which method to use are made by parents themselves. It is therefore inevitable that this outcome will be achieved, since the parent is given the role of 'expert' on their own child and family. This is particularly empowering to parents from different races or cultures who may otherwise feel that their own values and views are being overlooked.

Services are more appropriate to parents' needs

Andy Gill found, from his research, that there was a similarity and predictability in parental needs and experiences. Most parents, prior to joining a group, complained of isolation, confusion, helplessness and frustration in response to their children's behaviour. Parents expressed a wish to have an investment in prevention rather than crisis intervention. The fun and families group programme offers a preventative approach. In addition, through the process of evaluation (see Part V) parents are able to offer feedback to improve the services on offer. For example the Centre is developing a 'Parents' Manual' so that parents have a method of keeping all the handouts and booklets in a sturdy folder. This is in response to parents finding difficulty in keeping them all in one place or trying to keep prying hands or dogs' teeth off them!

Problem-solving skills are improved

It is evident from the evaluation results of successive fun and families groups that the average 50% reduction in child behaviour difficulties achieved by parents is a reflection of the increased problem-solving skills of parents who have attended a group. Examples of parents' comments on this include: 'I have learnt to look and handle situations differently; more positively, calmer, praising and talking,' and 'The course helped me to understand what was going on and how I could change it.'

A very common and understandable question about the evaluation results is whether the improved problem-solving skills are sustained over time. Andy Gill's research project involved interviewing and testing how well parents were retaining the progress they had made after three months, six months and every six months until three years had elapsed. His research showed that parents did continue to hold on to the progress made, although there was inevitably some degree of deterioration. There is a fuller discussion of the reasons for this and why certain parents seem to hold on to the progress better than others in Part IV.

One of the common criticisms of groupwork is that it does not change the status quo. However, there have been some interesting examples of how parents, having regained their sense of control and self-esteem, begin to tackle matters beyond child behaviour. One set of three parents who attended a fun and families group in Bradford all lived in council temporary accommodation. They came to recognise, during the process of the group, that they had gone as far as they could to improve their children's behaviour. However, their accommodation was hampering them because of poor conditions, including rotting and unsafe windows, leaking plumbing and a number of other faults. Consequently, the three parents wrote a joint letter asking for an appointment to see the Chair of the Housing Committee to request improvements to their housing conditions. This example demonstrates that the fun and families group programme can help parents to develop strategies for change beyond simply changing their children's behaviour, and therefore has the potential to change the status quo.

Greater diversity and choice of services develops to meet parents' needs more appropriately

The fun and families groupwork programme has developed from one programme to offer services to Asian parents, to a groupwork programme for parents of teenagers and a programme for parents with children with special needs. In addition the Centre has positively responded to parents' needs to have a female worker (Liz King) at the Centre.

Forward planning of services is based upon the best information and therefore more accurately reflects parents' needs

Information about parents' views are obtained from the feedback from evaluation forms, through discussions at parent support groups and from parents who serve on the Centre's governing body. From these sources changes and improvements have been made over the period the programme has been running.

Hopefully, this section on empowerment has given you a clear theoretical view of empowerment and offered you guidelines for the types of approach to running fun and families group that are likely to empower parents.

Anti-discriminatory practice

Anti-discriminatory practice has been defined as 'an approach to social work practice which seeks to reduce, undermine or eliminate discrimination and oppression, specifically in terms of challenging sexism, racism, ageism and disablism and other forms of discrimination encountered in social work' (Thompson, 1993, p. 31).

In this section it is intended to consider how such practice can be put into action while running a fun and families group. From a theoretical perspective, this can best be approached by looking at the positive action that an organisation, team or individual can aim to achieve in undertaking any social work task or activity. These positive actions can include:

- Raising awareness
- Working in partnership with others and acting collectively
- Having a clear theoretical base to work from
- Keeping anti-discriminatory practice as a central issue, not an optional or additional focus
- Being prepared to monitor, evaluate and be critical of your practice, and to learn and change in response to feedback.

With these theoretical guidelines for action it is helpful to look at how each of these positive actions can be achieved in the process of planning and running a fun and families group programme. It is worth repeating that these can only be general guidelines which need to take account of local conditions and circumstances. We have intended to use the list below as a checklist to be read in conjunction with Chapter 2, 'Practical lessons learned'. A number of positive actions can help achieve anti-discriminatory practice.

Raising awareness

When planning a fun and families group, the following ideas can be considered to raise awareness of issues of discrimination:

- Your publicity material can be a medium for offering positive images of people who suffer discrimination. This can be in terms of language, pictures or logos used.
- Home visits give an opportunity to refer to your organisation's anti-discriminatory practice policy.
- The locations where you might choose to run your groups can be used to raise awareness; for example, if you can select a venue that has facilities for people with disabilities.
- By planning to involve actively male partners in your group you are making a statement about men's equal responsibility for child care. Alternatively, running an all-female group and focusing on awareness raising and empowerment of women can change people's views.
- Planning to run groups for people of different races in your area is a good way to raise your agency's and your own awareness of their needs.
- In co-working with other agencies, anti-discriminatory practice can be promoted.

During the running of a fun and families group the following suggestions can be made to raise awareness:

- During the first session parents can be made aware of and can contribute to establishing the goals for the group which can include a commitment to anti-discriminatory practice. This can be reinforced in subsequent discussions in later sessions.
- Ensure that all hand-outs, videos, booklets, games and exercises offer positive images of people who suffer discrimination and contain no implicitly discriminatory material.
- Ensure that translations of written material are available. In addition co-work with colleagues who can interpret languages spoken by parents who live in your area, or arrange for interpreters/signers.

Working in partnership with others and acting collectively

The successful running of fun and families groups almost inevitably involves other workers and agencies. This is most likely to occur in either seeking premises, seeking a co-worker, providing child-care facilities or finding ways of publicising and seeking referrals for your group. Through your contact with such workers and agencies it is possible to support the efforts of others who want to practice in an anti-discriminatory way. Examples of this might include supporting a worker who has been trying to persuade their management committee to provide access to their premises for people with disabilities, or writing a letter of support for the continuation of a project you have worked with that provides services for black families.

Having a clear theoretical base to work from

It is very important to be able to explain clearly why you might choose a particular course of action when running a fun and families group. It is 'essential that practice be based upon a clear and explicit theory base in order to be able to swim against the dominant tide of discriminatory assumptions' (Thompson, 1993, p. 153). Thompson offers a good theoretical base in his book. Such a good theoretical base will give you insight, for example, when proofreading a hand-out from a colleague or co-worker stating 'because of "manpower" shortages it is a "black day" for the "disabled" and the "elderly", that this can be rewritten 'because of staff shortages it is a depressing day for people with disabilities and older people.'

In addition to the use of language, specific action, symbols, pictures, etc. need to be studied to ensure they do not undermine your anti-discriminatory message. We have also referred in other parts of this book to the fact that social learning theory is helpful in offering an objective way of assessing behaviour and choices about how such behaviour might be changed.

Keeping anti-discriminatory practice as a central focus

When running a fun and families group several steps can be taken to maintain anti-discriminatory practice as a central rather than as an additional focus:

- Drawing parents' attention to your policy in the first session, and then making sure that all your materials retain the theme of positive images of people who are discriminated against, will give anti-discriminatory practice a central focus.
- Co-working with people from disadvantaged groups is more likely to assist you in presenting material in an anti-discriminatory way.
- Make sure your agency has an anti-discriminatory practice policy and action plan: this is a useful way to keep the issue in a central position and can support your efforts to implement it.
- Ensure your agency has representatives from disadvantaged groups on its management committee and employs staff from such groups. The existence and operation of an equal opportunities policy will be important in this respect.
- Utilise a range of measures to make the fun and families groups you run accessible and relevant to people from disadvantaged groups. These can include translations of material, co-working with workers from disadvantaged groups and using appropriate, attractive publicity.
- Draw attention to those traditional child-rearing practices such as sex role stereotyping which are implicitly sexist.

Monitoring, evaluating and being critical of your practice

There are several steps that can be taken to improve your practice when running fun and families groups:

- Use feedback from parents' evaluation forms received at the end of groups to look at the range of ways that your anti-discriminatory practice can be improved.
- If your agency has an action plan for its anti-discriminatory practice policy the plan, if stated in measurable terms, can be reviewed regularly by your management committee, managers, team or colleagues. These reviews can then be used to look at ways in which practice can be improved and progress monitored.

- Give permission to your colleagues or co-workers to give you critical (but constructive!) feedback on your anti-discriminatory practice and vice versa.
- Finally, it is important to take achievable, measurable steps. Avoid vague, vastly over-optimistic and unrealistic targets.

4 Social learning theory

Applying the principles of basic social learning theory

Everyone consciously or otherwise, continually shapes and changes each other's behaviour. Social learning theory (SLT) has examined the factors at play in this process: if a more deliberate attempt to change any behaviour is to be undertaken, we have guidelines to direct our efforts productively.

SLT provides, for those who study its basic tenets, a greater choice and level of control over their own affairs. They can recognise the ways other people influence them. Then, if they have some objection, this knowledge provides a way of countering such control. The theory is scientific and like the theory of gravity, it applies universally without bias or prejudice regarding race, gender or disability. Because it always sets behaviours in context, it avoids labelling anybody as a 'problem'. It provides simply a means of identifying behaviours and the way they are maintained. It is for whoever uses these ideas to decide whether or not a given behaviour should be changed. It is very important that consideration is given to the following preliminary lines of thought before taking action:

- Whether or not the behaviour is perhaps a stage of a child's 'normal' development
- Whether it is ethical to change it
- Whether the family feel pressured by relatives or statutory agencies.

Although the theory itself may be free from bias or prejudice, people who work with families are not. It is, therefore, vitally important that workers using the theory do not make assumptions about the values and methods of child management being used by families of different races and cultures.

The ethical application of the theory must rest with the practitioner. This is because, as with atomic power or communication technology, the effectiveness is proven and powerful. Consequently, the care with which it is used is all the more important and the responsibility resting with those using it is so much greater.

The limitations of social learning theory

In practical terms SLT proposes that because behaviour is learned, it can therefore always be unlearned! Or, more significantly, an alternative can be learned to replace a behaviour judged to be unacceptable.

This brings a new perspective to many seemingly intractable and impossibly chaotic situations. The model simplifies intervention by providing just two alternatives:

1   It can identify behaviour which is not occurring as frequently as desired. Technically, this would be a behaviour 'deficit'. An example might be that a depressed person is not getting enough exercise. Well-tested principles and techniques can then be used to 'increase' the level of exercise. We can therefore increase behaviour which is not occurring frequently enough.
2   Alternatively, a behaviour may be performed 'in excess', occurring very often. This at times might be considered undesirable. Almost all young children throw temper tantrums. If this becomes an increasing pattern as they get older, it could be a grave social disadvantage. Learning how to control themselves is an essential social skill. Well-tested principles and techniques can then be used to decrease the frequency of tantrums. We can therefore decrease behaviour which occurs too often.

Learning how to define behaviour clearly

Step 1: describe the behaviour

First of all the behaviour must be precisely described: terms like 'naughty' or 'moody' are unhelpful. If we stop to think about such terms, each can embrace many behaviours. For example, 'naughty' might include hitting, spitting, whining, swearing, coming in late or not eating meals. 'Moody' might include not talking, not listening, being upset, crying or storming out of the room.

The skill of careful description is most important. Often it is the case, as with 'tantrums' above, that one behaviour leads to another. By dealing with one low-key behaviour (first in the hierarchy), other more stressful ones are nipped in the bud and prevented from becoming problems.

To check that our description is accurate, we ask other people involved what they understand by our definition of the behaviour they are trying to define more clearly. During our fun and families groups, parents do exercises in defining the behaviour they find difficulties with and want to change. They then check with other parents in the group if their description of the behaviour is clear. Provided everyone has the same perception, the actual words used are not so important. Once clear descriptions are agreed, it is probably sensible to choose just one or two behaviours to work with at first. This may seem as if the 'real problem' is being overlooked or trivialised. That is not the case. Serious reactive depressions have been overcome by simply getting a child to go to bed on time. This demonstrates how a simple task can resolve a really complex problem!

It is then necessary for parents to choose their target behaviours with care and really commit themselves to the task. It is easy to get distracted and let the first resolve erode. If parents have chosen well, and work at applying SLT precisely, there is every reason to believe change will occur. One success leads to another, and if more work needs doing, this will give confidence and enthusiasm to tackle the task.

Step 2: 'track' the behaviour

Studies have shown that 'tracking' behaviour is a crucial skill. In the everyday hurly-burly of life, many behaviours go unnoticed or are responded to inconsistently. Thus, sometimes swearing will be laughed at, ignored or chastised all in the same home by the same people. Doing something about it requires that these differing responses are noted and the time or context of the variations noticed. It has been found that people who learn to 'track' problem behaviours quickly resolve the difficulties they are experiencing.

A way of 'tracking' behaviour is to keep written records and charts. This makes the process so much easier and also enables progress to be monitored, which, in this type of work, is a great advantage. They can be used in two most important ways:

1   Therapeutically, it can be extremely important to demonstrate that progress is being achieved. Often those involved are too fraught to notice or feel the difference when initial small improvements occur. Therefore, charts and records actively demonstrate that progress is in fact happening.

2   Ethically, the adviser needs to realise how things are moving so that fine-tuning or changes to suggested programmes can be made.

Once records are kept, even for a short time, they often show that the behaviour to be changed is mainly confined to a given time or situation, perhaps at key points during the day such as bedtime, meal times or at a grandparent's! Finding out this type of information can help to concentrate efforts to change to a specific time-limited period, for example, a parent might then decide to improve difficult behaviour around meal times. It thus makes the task less onerous for parents by narrowing down the task to specific times and behaviours.

Another advantage of keeping records is that it can assist the learning process and consequent changes in behaviour. An example of this occurred at one of our fun and families groups when a parent noticed that when he left his lounge to fill in the chart about his child's crying, the noise stopped! So inadvertently, he learned to use the withdrawal of attention to the child to control problematic crying bouts.

If you have the equipment and feel comfortable with the idea, making audio or video recordings of behaviour can also be another very useful way of recording. Children respond well to seeing and hearing what they are really like! Quite often, it comes as a real shock to watch themselves communicating with their parents – a typical comment has been 'Did I really speak like that?' Another response has been that they just reflectively say nothing. Similarly, parents can also learn a thing or two about their own communication and responses. Video- and tape-recording, when used appropriately, does work much more effectively with young people. It is better than them feeling they are being 'lectured' to by their parents.

Discovering the context of the behaviour

The next stage is to begin to try and discover the context in which the difficult or problematic behaviour occurs. It is important at this stage to take time and effort over this part of the assessment and carefully collect as much information and detail about *what* is actually happening before rushing ahead and trying to make false guesses about *why* it is happening.

Step 1: identify the 'trigger'

Look for antecedents or triggers: events which come immediately before the selected behaviour. It is necessary to find out where, when, frequency and who is present at the time. These events are probably the stimuli to which the behaviour is a response. Stimuli are most significant in maintaining current behaviour as they provide an environment capable of suggesting, encouraging, instructing and offering ideas which can be copied or acted upon. Generally speaking, people love to copy. Modelling and copying behaviours provide a setting to show how something might be done and provide an opportunity to practice it. It may also suggest or prompt an action causing it to be repeated. For example, a shy child sees Lego on the TV and has ideas about what he or she would like to build. The child might then see other children playing with Lego in a public place and feel suitably interested to want to join in, but feel prevented by shyness. Perhaps with a little bit of prompting, the child will eventually pluck up the courage to join in. This process is known as modelling.

So, simply by adjusting the environment we can encourage behaviours by giving examples, opportunities and prompts. Similarly, if we remove these elements, the behaviour will be discouraged.

Step 2: observe the behaviour

Examine the selected behaviour and the very strong relationship it has to the antecedents which immediately precede it. If you strengthen or enhance the stimuli, you increase the behaviour. If you weaken or modify the stimuli, you decrease the behaviour.

At this stage, you may also notice the strong relationship the behaviour has with that which immediately follows it. These consequences or 'pay offs' for behaviour are discussed in Step 3.

Step 3: what follows the behaviour?

Carefully note the consequences or events which immediately follow the behaviour. Reinforcers, sometimes loosely referred to as 'pay offs', are events which occur just seconds, certainly no more than minutes, after the behaviour. During observation, you will soon notice how the child or young person being observed, will be encouraged by the response he or she receives, for example where a child screams and shouts and throws a temper tantrum in the shop in order to get a bar of chocolate. The parent, in desperation, gives in to the child's demands in order to avoid further embarrassment. Thus, the child's behaviour has been positively reinforced.

However, sometimes this can seem contradictory or to have the opposite effect. For example, a child's behaviour can be increased by receiving a slap from a parent who in fact is really hoping that it will stop the unwanted behaviour. This form of intense physical attention can be rewarding to some children because even a slap, or another form of physical abuse, is preferable to some children than being ignored. In addition, physical punishments can often be associated with shouting, chasing and general parental loss of control; all of which can be rewarding to the child.

You may also observe the way that behaviour is discouraged or inhibited. This can also appear contradictory. For example, some people find being the focus of attention or receiving hugs discomforting. They may then seek to avoid attracting such seemingly desirable acts by decreasing behaviour which may invite such responses. By definition, if a behaviour exists and is performed frequently, it is being reinforced. SLT assessment involves carefully seeking out sustaining or rewarding facets in the interactions between those involved. Also, if a behaviour is performed infrequently or is non-existent, it has probably been 'punished'. Therefore, the task is to identify those factors which are aversive or inhibiting to behaviour. This, in SLT terms, is known as the ABC Model of functional analysis, and stands for

Antecedent → Behaviour → Consequences.

If this is undertaken thoroughly, it provides a very good understanding of what maintains one given behaviour and what erodes another. This is commonly to do with the way people interact with each other.

Making plans for improvement

Step 1: be positive

Whenever possible, be positive. A very effective way of doing this is by turning the difficult behaviour on its head: rewarding a teenager for coming in early or on time, rather than having punishments for coming in late, is likely to work better. Another example might be that of rewarding loving or kind statements rather than trying to stop jealous ones. It is more enjoyable to administer and to receive positive approaches and it has been found in practice more likely that other behaviours will also change. This is probably because the joy of success encourages other improvements without additional work. It has also been found that the improvements hold up longer over time.

Step 2: have a clear goal

Be clear and single minded and know what you want to achieve. Remember that with SLT, you can either *increase* behaviour or *decrease* behaviour. Do not get sidetracked into looking for more involved explanations. Hold firm to the practical fact that often, by changing one or two behaviours, wider benefits are achieved. To achieve this you must focus on changing the selected target behaviour. This will be a demanding enough task in itself to achieve. So, examples here might be where a parent is complaining that the child will 'not do anything I ask', or, 'will not go to bed on time'. The clearly defined selected behaviour could be putting his toys away when asked by parent, or going to bed at 8pm each evening (age-appropriate, of course).

Then, an imaginative and enjoyable little programme or routine can be worked out that is rewarding for both the child and the parent.

Step 3: use punishment as a last resort

If some negative or troublesome behaviours cannot be changed, more punishing techniques can be used with caution. The problem, however, is that they have the potential to backfire on you. Physical punishment has a law of diminishing returns and quickly teaches the recipient to avoid getting caught rather than to amend their ways. It also creates tension and dislike between those involved. Quite often the use of physical punishment means that parents have to resort to slapping a bit harder each time because it is not having the desired effect. Relationships can rapidly break down and the parent becomes more and more desperate. Even those techniques used for reducing unwanted behaviour which are less upsetting, nonetheless, do not teach what you want to happen. Therefore, a kind of vacuum is created, because neither child or parents know what they really want to achieve or what is expected.

It is probably best therefore to use 'punishing' techniques only as a last resort and always together with other 'positive' strategies. This cannot be over-stressed. Quite often, once parents get into 'punishing' techniques, the more positive strategies just get lost and forgotten about. It is very important to try and make a benign and positive package of techniques.

This is particularly relevant when parents are having to use 'time out'. This technique can be very effective in controlling extreme temper tantrums. But, it has to be used in combination with a strong rewarding programme for the child attempting the desired or 'good' behaviour. Hopefully, this will gradually replace the need for lost temper.

Tools of the trade: ways of changing behaviour

There are many good books which contain a comprehensive range of available techniques, some of which are listed at the end of this book. By using more than one reference, you can get an overall view and avoid what can often be a 'cook book' approach. A good range of techniques are essential and their use can only be accurate if the assessment is carefully undertaken.

Each technique has a specific purpose. For example, the technique of 'time out' is effective for extreme attention-seeking behaviour, whereas 'overlearning' is more effective in dealing with avoidance behaviours. A child throwing things could be employing behaviour to get attention or to create a diversion as a way of avoiding an unpleasant task such as tidying up.

The assessment identifies the nature of the individual difficult or problematic behaviour. The worker then helps parents determine which are the most appropriate methods and techniques to use.

When trying to increase behaviour, ensure that the child or young person knows exactly what is expected of him or her. This can involve far more than what we first think. We must not assume they know what is expected or that they can actually do the task. Therefore, a successful change plan will include:

1   Clear guidelines which are fully understood by and acceptable to all concerned.
2   Task-modelling to ensure the skill exists to achieve what is required. This may require role play, practising and correcting minor errors, and checking to ensure there is some resolve with the carer or child to accomplish the task.
3   Reinforcements or rewards for the achievement of small steps or approximations such as putting on socks, trousers, shoes, etc. Every individual step should be rewarded.

Effective reinforcers

The most effective forms of reinforcers are

- Social rewards such as hugs, smiles, cuddles – these have been shown to be the most powerful and long-lasting.
- Social activities or shared outings – these can include reading books with parents, playing games or going on outings. Again these are very strong reinforcers and also aid good communication between parents and children.
- Money and 'goodies' – these are the least effective by themselves, although they can have a very short-term effectiveness. They are useful tokens though, and make a total package more manageable and interesting for the child. Care is needed to avoid getting into agreements which involve expensive financial rewards.

It needs to be stressed here that the above three points are generalised statements and care needs to be taken that due consideration, respect and thought is given to the family's race, culture and religious needs. It is also worth bearing in mind a child's history. For example, a foster child from a very disadvantaged background may not find cuddles or hugs reinforcing if they have never experienced them, or if they have previously been sexually abused.

Effective forms of decreasing behaviour

Reinforce an alternative behaviour

This is the most powerful method. Parents often come to a group wanting to decrease a behaviour in their child which they are very concerned about, for example, the child may be biting themselves or others, setting fire to the carpet or throwing knives. The aim of choosing an alternative behaviour to work on is to prevent the focus of attention all going towards the biting, knives, etc. If the targeted behaviour is, 'to reduce Dean's biting of other children', then, the whole idea of biting is still being focused on. If, instead, the targeted behaviour chosen is, ' for Dean to play with another child for two minutes or more each day', then it can be seen that the focus is turned away from Dean's biting. The targeted behaviour now becomes a more 'rewarding' and positive one which is more effective in the long run for both parent and child. Sometimes it is difficult to persuade parents and carers to agree to something which feels like they are being asked to reward someone for being 'bad'! However, what we need to stress here is that we are rewarding specific behaviour, rather than the individual as a person.

Ignoring

This can also be very powerful but sometimes tricky to achieve, as often problems arise when good behaviour is ignored unintentionally. An almost ritual regime may need to be used for a while to establish a changed pattern of responses, for example, turning away dramatically, showing your back to the child, and walking firmly off the scene. For some very destructive behaviour, this technique is only advisable if a partner or friend is around to make sure the child or property is not at risk.

Withdrawing benefits or privileges

Items such as pocket money, outings, sweets or stopping-out later are removed from the child for unwanted behaviour. The child needs to be fully aware of what is being removed and why it is being removed. It is only then that he or she can take responsibility for their action. Like all of these more 'punishing' techniques, they are open to misuse. It can be easy to remove the whole week's pocket money, stop the outing which the whole family has been looking forward to, or lock the new bicycle away in the shed for a month. The child then has nothing to work towards with such punishments and can therefore give up. The aim therefore is to remove only a small part of the benefit or privilege.

Response cost

This technique can be used to show that there is a *cost* to undesirable behaviour. It places responsibility for some unpleasant consequences firmly upon the young person's own shoulders. This takes on many guises – from the denial of pocket money or fines to elaborate token economies. With the latter, tokens, marbles, beans or any imaginative device can be used to reward a child. These can be saved up and exchanged for other more tangible items such as trips out with a parent, sweets, small amounts of money or perhaps having a friend for tea. Sometimes these tokens can be used to teach more subtle lessons.

Bonus tokens can be given for meeting expected targets which can then be removed if predetermined unacceptable behaviour occurs. This teaches that individual performance can earn both advantages and penalties. In technical terms, these are called 'response cost' programmes. When removing tokens, it is important that only bonus tokens are removed as penalties. It is very important that too much should not be lost too easily, for example, when all of a young person's pocket money is removed and he or she has nothing to work towards. When young people are in no-win situations they can become unpredictable and negative.

'Time out'

This technique can be controversial for some people. However, it is very effective and much researched, so that new details are emerging all the time. 'Time out' works by removing rewarding (reinforcing) influences. This means that the behaviour will be deprived of encouragement and will reduce in frequency. It may involve removing a child from a room, or being made to face a blank wall. With adolescents or some children, it may be easier for the parent or carer to remove themselves. The objective is to avoid giving attention to a behaviour you wish to discourage. Some would suggest no more than three to five minutes should be endured in 'time out' for any child. Others suggest one minute for each year of the child's age but not more than five minutes.

We would always stress that this technique is used as a last resort if all else fails. The reason for this is that it is easy to use it wrongly and therefore cause additional problems. Also, families need help throughout the process and should not be left alone to administer 'time out'. It can be very stressful for parents until success is achieved. Generally speaking, the more positive techniques described above usually achieve desired results so, in practice, there is rarely a need to use this method which is why we mention it last of all.

Finally, always encourage parents to keep records throughout the entire intervention. It is worth the effort even if it seems like an extra chore. It makes it possible to take responsibility for whatever change is being achieved and can be comforting and reassuring to people. Quite often they appreciate the integrity and attention to detail. Records also show when decisions are made about when to change intervention. A further reason for keeping records is because we know from research that initially, an attempt to change a behaviour can, perhaps for several days, lead to an increase in the behaviour. This is because the child has developed a habit or pattern of behaviour and the child may regard the parent's changed response as temporary. Only when the child sees an ongoing change in either the antecedents or consequences of the behaviour will a sustained and rapid reduction in the behaviour occur. Without accurate records, a parent may, after two or three days of trying a new approach with no apparent success, conclude that the strategy does not work. Finally, keeping records also takes the mystique out of the relationship between parents and the worker and avoids unnecessary feelings of dependency.

5 The role of cognitive behavioural theory

Introduction

What we see and what we tell ourselves can have a profound effect upon how we feel and therefore on how we work and play. Everybody at times interprets what they see in a narrow or unhelpful fashion. If this is not recognised it can lead to a vicious downward cycle of gloom or ineffective action. Many of the parents who attend our groups identify with this cycle. One parent wrote, 'I used to think that I was a terrible mother and that my children were little devils compared to most other kids. Having talked to other parents on the course I can now see that my difficulties are not as unusual or as bad as I thought and this helps.'

Although the fun and family courses are designed to encourage parents to discover their own expertise in managing their children's behaviour, sometimes in addition to this a profound change takes place in the way they look at things and how they feel about themselves.

It can be helpful to identify when our own, or other people's, thinking is leading to unhelpful feelings. Thinking can fuel action which makes situations worse as well as evoking uncomfortable feelings. If it is possible to see the stars from a prison, of whatever kind, an escape is already half-way planned. Within the course of the group programme, parents frequently begin to see an escape route for themselves. Cognitive behaviour theory helps us facilitate that process. Not only is it useful to further our own understanding about what group members are struggling with, but also some of the concepts can be shared with course members, as they provide useful coping strategies. It also fills out our perspective and provides tools to deal with material which straightforward behaviour-changing strategies cannot always address.

Recognising negative thinking

It is very easy to hear other people running themselves down: 'I can't cope', 'I have never been any good at organising things.' It is equally easy to see the unhelpful nature of such statements and feel an urge to rush in with comforting reassuring words.

The problem with such reassurance is that it will probably not achieve anything, because the person who habitually says something like 'I can't cope' quite probably believes it to be the absolute truth. Another possibility is that they do not realise just how often they say it, and how pervasive and influential such thinking is for them. In other words, they do not hear themselves constantly repeating unhelpful ideas. For these reasons, among others, remonstrating with them will be irrelevant.

The first task is therefore to identify accurately the more acutely unhelpful thoughts. Then try to demonstrate their link with bad feelings and unhappy outcomes.

A simple model, which can almost be used like a party game is captured in the following grid:

Event	Belief	Feeling	Outcome
Loss of job	I'm useless	depression	do nothing/no new job

Frequently, things happen which make us feel anxious. In these days of huge unemployment many, even if they try, will not get a job. Without in any way underestimating the very real distress such events create, it is important to grasp that it is not the kind of thinking which lies behind temporary or passing events which we would want to challenge. It is normal and necessary, for example, to mourn the loss of a loved one, or a job, and feel wretched in the process. What we are looking for is interpretations of events which pervade a person's whole thinking and make them habitually dissatisfied and unhappy.

One mother had it fixed in her mind that her two young boys, about seven and nine years old, were 'just like their dad!'. Their dad had raped and beaten her on many occasions before she had separated from him. So everything the children did was seen through this filter, and was taken to be a deliberate attempt to hurt her. She became so anxious that she was afraid to chastise them, and believed that even their kind actions had ulterior motives – if they helped with the washing-up, which they often did, her response was 'what are they after'.

The grid above has its limitations because it only deals with one or two situations, in isolation. Difficulties arise when somebody consistently views themselves as 'useless' or 'hopeless' and relates those stock appraisals to a wide range of different situations. Using the grid to work a number of examples can serve two purposes. It identifies clearly what is being said by the person in their ruminations, as their automatic response to many situations. It also begins the process of helping them to make links between thinking and feeling and the ability to get on with life in an interesting satisfying manner.

Filling in the grid can start with writing down either the feeling first, or the failure to act, or the belief or event – the order does not matter. What is important is the sense of the difference between these elements and their relationship to each other. Differentiating between thoughts and feelings can sometimes be very difficult, after all, we describe our feelings with words which we also use to share our thoughts. Unhelpful thoughts can be recognised by a number of characteristics.

It is not ordinary statements of disappointment or understandable anxiety that would be selected as targets to work with. Unhelpful thoughts are *not true* as they stand, because they are either

- Generalisations e.g., the person in the grid may be useless at their job, but it is unlikely they are useless at everything, which is what 'I am useless' says, or
- Exaggerations, such as the above example of the mother's view of her little boys. They were not for instance as big and strong as their father, or
- Extreme evaluations, like a student who felt it was unbearable not to be awarded a first class honours degree because it implied he was unworthy to live or succeed in anything, or
- Inferences which draw conclusions far beyond what the evidence can stand. An example would be 'my child always comes in late at night (probably fact) because he knows I worry and he wants to upset me' (the inference).

'MUSTturbatory' thinking is a term coined by Albert Ellis (see Dryden and Golden, 1986, p. 16). It describes thinking which ascribes moral absolutes to every area of life – it insists, for example, 'I *must* do well', in order to be liked; 'You *must* treat me fairly', otherwise I shall not be able to bear it; 'The world *must* be fair', if not that is a major disaster and catastrophic.

Dysfunctional thinking will contain the seeds of emotional discomfort, maladaptive behaviour and leave the owner of such thoughts feeling self-defeated. In other words, some things we tell ourselves get in the way of attaining the personal goals we would otherwise choose.

Change is possible

Even songs – '*Que sera sera*, whatever will be will be' – din into us that we have no control, that beliefs are fixed and cannot be changed, that we have to suffer what life throws at us. An important step towards change is often to start showing that there are different ways of thinking. From the grid below we see that a different interpretation of the same situation is possible. It is helpful to generate as many examples as possible, but not expect the 'sufferer' to change their mind ... yet! Just get them to see alternatives.

Event	Belief	Feeling	Outcome
Loss of job	I'm useless	depression	do nothing
	it's the recession	anger: I'll fight this	search for work

Patiently demonstrate that it is possible to change quite deep-seated thought patterns if the evidence is convincing. Common examples: most people surrender belief in Father Christmas; most have stopped believing the world is flat! Just establish the principal that people do change their minds. Finally, select an unhelpful thought to change; this task requires skill and it is essential to be very clear which thought is to be the focus of work. In our groups, parents become familiar with selecting behaviours to change. Inadvertently, we see in them a gradual, sometimes dramatic change in their point of view, and sense of well-being. This is because the work they do is already challenging some of their preconceptions which have hindered progress before. Once they regain control over some of their children's more troublesome behaviour, the tendency to keep telling themselves that they are hopeless and have no control is less credible and influential.

We all indulge in personal monologues, appraising and interpreting our situation through our own individual filters. Aaron Beck (1976) calls this process having 'automatic thoughts'. These instruct our daily activities and more importantly our feelings. He suggests that work can be done with these thoughts which are not necessarily deep-seated.

Albert Ellis (1973) places more emphasis on the concept that everyone has a quite limited, but deep-seated and significant set of 'core beliefs'; the most effective way of helping is to tease out these specific core beliefs as the subject for change. His style is more probing and confrontational than Beck's.

One way of describing this process is to say that such thoughts have been 'overlearned'. For example, to 'be seen and not heard' was a common requirement for children in past generations. That may not be too troublesome a rule in a young person's life. However, as an adult it is both inhibiting and embarrassing. Being subject to such a rule could cause blushing, stuttering or even more debilitating responses from an individual who longs to speak out among adult peers, but is stuck with this 'overlearned' belief, which is no longer appropriate, but still holds its power.

A book by S. Walen *et al.* (1980) describes how to tease out appropriate target thoughts. In another text, by McMullin and Giles (1981), it is suggested that the creation of 'cognitive maps' can be an aid to identifying troublesome thoughts. This involves listing 10–20 different situations which have resulted in discomfort. Then use the grid to focus which thoughts lie behind those upsetting situations. If they are carefully examined and shaped into personal statements about oneself, it is usually discovered that only half a dozen or so different themes appear.

When doing this analysis, it is important that the person wanting to change does their own work. The group worker's task is to lead them to find answers which genuinely relate to their own circumstances. 'Socratic dialogue' is a term used to describe a collaborative style of question-and-answer which enables a person to arrive at their own conclusions. This is very important, bearing in mind that advice is unlikely to be believable to someone stuck with unhelpful cognitions. Trying to force the pace, or do the work for someone, is not likely to work well. It is clear that great sensitivity towards the individual's culture, religion, sexual orientation, disability and circumstances would be a prerequisite in using these ideas in individual work. For example, someone saying 'It is my duty' may not be displaying an unhelpful cognition.

One way of assessing which are the most potent thoughts is to use a rating system in which each thought is measured on a scale of 1–10 according to the level of distress caused. These distress levels are called SUDS (Subjective Units of Distress). This can be useful in selecting which thought to begin challenging. It also provides a continuing measure of progress. Other measures of movement can be used in conjunction with this. Self-report, friends' reports, direct observation about dress and body posture can provide indicators about progress. Use as many forms of feedback as possible. The person struggling to change strong habits of thinking can find these most encouraging.

Overleaf is a chart of the results of one particular piece of work, which happily produced significant change: 10 represents the worst level of distress. Although there were fluctuations in scores as work progressed, with some individual thoughts seemingly getting an even firmer hold, overall the situation gradually improved.

Thoughts	Monthly SUDs Ratings			
	Month 1	Month 2	Month 3	Month 4
I can't cope	5	5	2	0
I'm not wanted	2	2	2	0
I'm not likeable	5	2	0	1
Everyone is better than me	2	3	2	1
My boys are like their dad!	10	8	9	3
Total scores for first five thoughts	24	20	15	5
My boys want to hurt me	–	6	8	4
I feel useless	–	7	5	2
Total scores for all seven thoughts	24	33	28	11

Bringing about change

Keep firmly in mind that the objective is to enable the subject to feel better, be more emotionally buoyant, and be free of debilitating physical symptoms of anxiety or depression. Dispute, counter or challenge those thoughts which have been identified as having a strong influence upon the person's feelings and general sense of well-being. This process involves eroding maladaptive thoughts and replacing them with constructive appraisals. Gradually, establish the new helpful beliefs as habit, make them an automatic response to stressful situations.

The measure of success is thus rather different from that used in behavioural interventions. Success is essentially to do with the extent to which the client 'feels' better. Behaviour can change without achieving this. One client, for example, successfully ran a programme to overcome her children's soiling problem. It was intended as a counter to her pervasive cognition that she could not cope. However, she felt no pleasure whatever in the change and could not see how her own ability had helped to bring it about. It was therefore not a successful project and others had to be devised.

One of the claims for cognitive behaviour work is that, because it deals with a person's own sense of worth and achievement, it has a greater generalising effect than simple behavioural work. However, it is quite complex and a great deal of information emerges in the process. Consequently when working in this way the helper needs to keep a very firm grasp of the thoughts they are attempting to change if they are to avoid confusion, or draw the wrong conclusions about progress.

Another thing to be aware of is that the target thoughts will quite frequently be very firmly established, that is, 'overlearned'. An intellectual move is likely to occur in advance of any significant emotional change. It takes time for the new thinking to become automatic and have a predictable influence upon the feelings. The example used earlier about being taught as children to 'be seen and not heard' illustrates this point. When they grow up, if this has been overlearned, they still feel uncomfortable when challenging other adults, perhaps blushing or feeling stupid. It can be comparatively easy to realise intellectually that adults need to speak up for themselves, and have their own view of things. What is difficult is establishing that awareness to the extent that it helps them feel comfortable when expressing their own strongly held views. The only way is to keep practising, repeating the new thinking and trying it out. The discomfort is unavoidable, motivation comes from knowing the reasonableness of such a strategy and keeping the long-term goal in mind.

Unhelpful thoughts can be changed using three broad strategies.

Logical or rational dispute

This involves assembling as much evidence as possible which contradicts the target thought. It may be the thought as it stands is challenged and redefined. For example, 'I can't cope' is analysed and shown to be a very general statement which might be true as an expression of feeling, but is not fact. If areas where the person can cope (manage money, cook, dance well) can be identified, these should be written down and rehearsed. Gradually, 'I can't cope' as a basic tool of personal appraisal is seen to be inaccurate and can be replaced with a more positive accurate view.

Other evidence contradicting the target thought might be expert opinions, or written work, and research. The most effective evidence will be that which the individual can self-generate. This needs to be in strong contrast to the unhelpful thought. The mother who saw her boys as being just like their father created a list of things they did which were thoughtful and gave her pleasure. She also itemised all the differences in physical and emotional make-up they had which set them apart from their father. 'Not coping' would be better countered by noticing things done really well, than by marginal competence. The counters need to be concise so that they can be rehearsed daily, perhaps recorded on a prompt card as an aid to the memory. Above all *they must be believed* by whomever is using them.

Practical tasks

Sometimes it is necessary to take some risks and actually do something which shows the thought to be untrue. If someone suffering from agoraphobia actually goes out alone and survives (which they always do), they realise that saying 'I can't go out, the panic would kill me' is less than the whole story. One mother believed if she stayed away from her home for a night her teenage children would wreck the house with wild partying. She was persuaded to put this to the test and learned that it was not true. She also discovered that she enjoyed getting away from home, and that the teenagers behaved better being left to their own devices and having some responsibility, than they had when she was always keeping an eye on them.

It is here that confusion can creep in: the object of these tasks was not to demonstrate a social skill and count that successful. Developing a wider range of interests outside the home was helpful, but the intention was to demonstrate that the fearful stories she told herself and the consequent anxiety were not based in fact. The point of the exercise is to see if the belief is dislodged and the person feels better about themselves.

Role-playing or practising proposed tasks may be an important preliminary for some people if they are going to take on an assignment with any confidence and hope of success.

Arousal control

Panic or acute anxiety can make the mind so agitated or the body so uncomfortable that planned action becomes impossible. If this is likely, strategies to demonstrate control should be practised. Deep muscle relaxation can show just how much control is possible. Then there are many and various strategies which can be practised to establish more control. It is a question of 'horses for courses', finding what is useful for the individual. Meditation, graded relaxation, or listening to music are just some of the things which could be tried to help alleviate intense morbid rumination.

There are strategies to be used in emergencies if the above have become second nature. Thought stopping – twanging a rubber band against the wrist, or counting to ten, followed by rehearsing a positive statement – can be used to break into ruminations. One client used the rubber band to avoid panic at the start of driving lessons and even used it during her driving test to quell panics, happily with a successful outcome.

Deep breathing, or other individual rituals all have a role if chosen appropriately. Any of the above counters need to be undertaken with some spirit, intense conviction, assertion and even personal internal aggression.

Change in the groupwork programme

In our groupwork programmes we spend very little time working formally with the above model. However, it is most interesting to observe the process and principles described. Even though the participants are not aware of it, the stories they tell themselves change as the course progresses. Examples include those who start the course declaring 'I can't cope', but end feeling quite positive about themselves and their ability. What happens? Well, they share the unhelpful thoughts with other parents, who by their comments and examples gradually show them to be inaccurate. They discover very competent, coping people, struggling with rampant toddlers just as they do, but notice that not everyone blames themselves or believes they are 'non copers' because of that.

In devising tasks to restore control to defeated parents, the group not only changes their own and their children's behaviour but in the process gives them experience and practice which challenges defeatist thinking. Our emphasis on making the work positive and fun creates a more relaxed attitude – even just coming out regularly from home to have space for oneself interrupts what has often become a very agitated lifestyle. So again this provides experience which, even without drawing attention to what is happening, in fact challenges thinking and alters feelings. The course is a great *stress reducer*.

The ideas can be used more formally in a one-to-one situation but there are certain things which need attending to, to ensure success. Individual work requires a heavy commitment on the part of worker and client. A guideline, offered by McMullin and Giles in 1981, is that it takes five sessions to complete an assessment, possibly another twelve sessions to complete intervention. They suggest the sessions should not be more than a week apart. D. Schulyer (1991), in his practical little book, itemises more flexible and varied schedules to meet people's individual needs and circumstances.

The home tasks are crucial: if they are not completed, check that they are understood and practical. Always be prepared to troubleshoot. Selecting appropriate target beliefs is essential – if progress is slow, it may be because this has not been done, or explained thoroughly enough.

Apart from working for change, the model is useful to help us judge more sensitively what is happening with people we meet and work with. Victims of child abuse routinely say to themselves things like, 'it was my fault', 'I must protect (the abuser)'. If we listen carefully we shall hear ourselves and others saying things, passing comment, framing personal perceptions which are unhelpful. We can then perhaps begin to sense how these comments, so much a part of an individual's repertoire, affect the way they feel and therefore perform. Knowledge of the model can also show

how useless advice, like 'pull oneself together' or 'snap out of it' is. It should offer us ideas about how to gently search for accurate information and subtly lead a person. It will take time before they can make more helpful ideas their own, and replace the handicapping cognitions they may have lived with for years.

This chapter is intended to be only a taster to what is a huge subject. It informs our practice generally, and is a very useful tool in developing a sensitive approach to those in some difficulty.

In the fifth session we find that parents enjoy using the 'ABCO' grid (see p. 104). They relate to the ideas and find that searching for alternative cognitions is useful to them. The way we use the grid directly with parents in the groupwork programme is set out more thoroughly in Chapter 9.

There is a vast literature on the subject. We have included some titles in the Reference section for further reading which we have found helpful, some of which have been referred to in the course of this chapter.

6 Groupwork skills: giving structure to groups for parents

Introduction

Running fun and families groups involves a combination of three essential skills:

- A sound grasp of social learning theory, the core of this being described in Chapter 4 'The basics of social learning theory' (also available in booklet form).
- Good planning to ensure that you attract a sufficiently large group of parents. A checklist for this is set out in Chapter 2, 'Planning a fun and families group' (also available in booklet form).
- A sense of how to structure the sessions of the groupwork programme so that they have a constructive purpose with clear goals, whilst being flexible enough to deal with the worries and anxieties of each parent.

It is with this last skill, that of being able to offer a clear structure, that we focus on in this chapter. The emphasis will be on the means of doing this, rather than on the actual content of each of the sessions. The outline and content of each session is comprehensively outlined in Part III.

The role of the group leader

In training sessions we have run on setting up and running groups for parents we have focused on the following as essential elements of the group leader's role:

- Create an informal, non-threatening and humorous working atmosphere. This can be encouraged in the first session by providing tea, coffee, biscuits or a glass of wine and a friendly atmosphere in which getting to know each other is a high priority. This probably seems like an obvious point but it is very evident that parents do feel very threatened by attending a group. This is clear from the feelings that parents have described to us in later sessions. A summary of these feelings is provided at the end of this chapter under the heading of 'Parents' feelings when they first attend a group'. Studying these comments should help group leaders plan methods of making parents feel at ease. Some ideas are also given in our booklet 'Games and exercises used in fun and families groups' and in Part III of this book.
- It is very evident that people of different races, cultures and religions, and disabled people will respond positively or negatively to different approaches. A good discussion of these issues is set out in *Race, Gender and Class* (Davis & Proctor, 1989).
- Set goals for each session. Our early experience suggests that you should not be over-optimistic about what you can get through in a two-hour session.
- Ensure everyone has a say and is involved – this requires helping to avoid people dominating or diverting from the goals of the session. The object of the group is to allow parents to achieve an understanding of children's behaviours while allowing them the opportunity to select and practice the methods they want to use to influence those behaviours. Again, because of the diversity of approaches that are acceptable to people of different races, cultures or religions, it is important to avoid a 'Eurocentric' approach, that is, a tendency to ignore or devalue any aspect of social, cultural or religious behaviour that is not basically white, European, and Christian.
- It is important at the start for group leaders to set the ground rules by stating their commitment to anti-discriminatory practice. This then allows group leaders to challenge sexist or racist remarks if they arise during group sessions.
- Give positive encouragement to everyone's efforts; be clearly encouraging and don't ignore or talk over people's responses. In particular, avoid any response that might be viewed as negative or threatening to parents. The building-up of informal support and confidence amongst group members is a vital task for group leaders.
- Regularly refer people to the underlying theoretical principles. This can be done through the use of small group exercises and games. Parents find it easier to apply the theoretical examples when they are applied to individual circumstances. The use of exercises also helps to identify individuals who may be lost or confused.

- Use your knowledge of group members to know when to help, for example, with difficulties with literacy. (This information will be available to you from your pre-group home visits.). Also, invite people to share their positive experiences with the group.
- Use a range of interesting materials: video, articles, case examples, role play. Good material encourages participation, should have practical relevance to parents and should ideally assist parents to practice parenting skills. Good material should also be non-sexist or non-racist. Poor material is usually too theoretical, has little practical relevance and, if done individually (rather than in pairs or small groups) fails to encourage group cohesion.
- Home tasks need to be negotiated at the end of each session and time given at the start of each subsequent session for feedback. This allows and encourages mutual support, problem solving and the growth of confidence. A good example of this was a parent who insisted that her 7-year-old son did not like cuddles and would wither in shame if she kissed him goodbye at the school gate. When she shared with the group (at the start of Session 3) that she had discovered that he did like cuddles and he had actually initiated kissing her goodbye at the school gate, her delight and dramatic growth in confidence was an inspiration to the rest of the group.
- Always evaluate each session and each group to find out what went right or wrong.
- Have fun!

We have found from experience that achieving all these aims is an impossible task for one group leader and we would strongly recommend the use of two group leaders, both of whom have been involved in the planning of the group and are comfortable in working together. We have indicated in Chapter 2, 'Planning a fun and families group', that it is helpful to have female and male co-leaders and also black workers where groups are being run for or include black families.

Basic procedures for discussion groups

Martin Herbert, in his book *Working with Children and their Families* (1988), describes a set of useful procedures for running parent groups. I have adapted these procedures to make them specifically relevant to fun and families groups:

- *Define terms and concepts* Groups require a shared language to hold a purposeful discussion. Words like 'discipline', 'punishment', 'problem behaviour' all have specific meanings within social learning theory as opposed to their everyday use. It is helpful, therefore, to find agreement and to give examples, where possible, to illustrate a word or a concept's meaning.

- *Negotiate and/or establish goals*   Clarify the goals or objectives of every session (see Part III for the contents of each session). Allow time for 'homework' tasks to be discussed and where possible relate these to the learning tasks for each session.
- *Encourage free and fair discussion*   Encourage individuals in the free (but fair) expression of ideas, feelings, attitudes, openness, reactions, information and analysis. Do not allow the scapegoating or bullying of any one member. Ground rules about confidentiality, racism, sexism and the importance of everyone having a say should usefully be agreed at the group's outset.
- *Integrate the material*   Continually refer to the learning that has been achieved over succeeding group sessions. The groupwork sessions are designed to gradually build up the parents' understanding of children and their confidence in their parenting skills.
- *Encourage the application of the discussion material*   Ask group members to identify the relevance of the learning material to their own lives. Encourage them to apply the positive things and report back to the group the 'feedback' they received from their efforts.

Effective group intervention

A group intervention will be effective if the following criteria are met:

- The group *climate* should be warm, accepting and non-threatening.
- Learning should be seen as a *co-operative* activity.
- *Learning* should be seen as the primary purpose of the group.
- Every member of the group should *participate*.
- Group sessions should be stimulating and *pleasurable*.
- *Evaluation* should be seen as a central part of the group's activities.
- Participants should come *regularly* and be prepared.

Troubleshooting – dealing with individual contributions

Even if all the points raised above have been attended to, often some situations arise that require confident but sensitive handling. The most common ones can include:

- People who go on at length, restricting the time left for others.
- People who drift off the main point to matters that are interesting but are outside the scope of the group.
- People who tend to dominate the rest of the group.
- People who start up private, secondary conversations during group discussions.
- People who make no (or very minimal) contribution to the group.

If these problems occur it is worth considering the points set out in the paragraph above on effective group intervention. For example, if the group climate has for some reason become 'threatening' or creates anxiety for parents it would be a reasonable response for parents to feel unwilling to contribute. A useful thought as far as troubleshooting is concerned is to work on the assumption that 'the best solutions are those you find before you have got the problem'. In other words, good planning and attention to the procedures referred to in the paragraphs above *should* help you to avoid having to become involved in anything more than minor troubleshooting!

The co-leader has an important role in watching for problems and intervening where they think necessary and also in supporting the other group leader's attempts to do so. The leaders should also consider strategies to cope with these difficulties in their planning meetings between each group session. The importance of ensuring everyone has a say is a vital role for the group leaders and should be stressed at the outset of each session when feedback on the weekly task is sought.

Where group leaders need to intervene to curtail someone's contribution, this needs to be done sensitively without causing offence. This requires the use of a range of skills which most of us practice every day without thinking about it:

- Initially, it is important to get eye contact with the person speaking.
- If this can't be done simply by looking at them, try a more active method such as standing up, moving to the flip chart or video, dropping a book or a pen, etc. to attract their attention.
- Once you have their attention, always give a positive reason for interrupting them (e.g., need to let everyone have a say, or need to move on to the next session) and thank them (where relevant) for their contribution.
- If people have individual matters they wish to raise that are not relevant to the group task, offer to see them at the end of the session so that the group as a whole can proceed.

If one individual has a persistent pattern of behaviour that continues to affect the group it is preferable to see them on their own to discuss this. Our experience has been that if such problems are not tackled by the group leaders, the group participants will deal with it, and often in a less sensitive and more critical manner.

Troubleshooting – strategies for groups

Groups that are stuck

By 'stuck' we mean that the group, or a proportion of the group, finds some aspect of the theoretical material difficult to accept. For example, one group found it hard to accept that recording behaviour on the Recording Charts would have any beneficial effect. If groups become 'stuck' it is most likely to happen in Sessions 1–3 because, at this stage, there is a high level of belief that 'nothing will work'. In addition any beneficial changes will not have started to show sustained success at this point.

The best approach in this situation is to press on with the programme, making sure that all the theoretical ideas have been rigorously covered. At the same time it is important to *acknowledge* the reservations expressed without becoming defensive.

In the example given above of the group that doubted the effectiveness of recording, an insight by a parent at the start of Session 2 helped them to move on. The parent concerned chose the task of noting down when his daughter cried, which he had identified as occurring when he sat down in the living room to read the paper. After a couple of days his daughter ripped up his chart so he got a fresh one and pinned it to the fridge in the kitchen to avoid losing a second chart. Every time she cried he went out to the kitchen to record the behaviour. After two to three days he noticed that the crying had stopped and he came back to Session 2 impressed by the power of recording.

Groups that become negative or defensive

A negative group is one in which the group members predominantly report no progress. It can often be a feature in small groups of 4–6 people that one person, who is making no progress, is very dominant. Obviously, some of the strategies referred to in the preceding section on troubleshooting with individuals are relevant here. In addition, as with 'stuck' groups, it also tends to be a feature of the first 2–3 sessions.

The best way to help such groups is based on the old adage 'Nothing succeeds like success'. This strategy might involve the following action. Find a parent who has obviously had some success and then let them start the feedback session, thereby creating a positive mood. In addition, during the feedback, seek out any success that some of the parents (who are experiencing negative results) have had and be very positive about this. It is also worth asking parents who are having some success to suggest some ideas to those who are not.

If a parent is clearly in great difficulties it can pay dividends to offer some individual help between sessions in order to help them achieve some success, however limited. Just as with 'stuck' groups, we have never known a group to be negative for the whole seven sessions, so pressing on with the programme while acknowledging the difficulties usually achieves the desired improvements in child behaviour.

Groups that lack cohesion, or have groups within the group

The mix of people who come to fun and families groups is usually a very positive feature and all seem to benefit from the diversity of backgrounds. However, on occasion, the group can fail to be mutually supportive or a small clique can develop within the group. Again a range of strategies need to be used:

- Make sure everyone has a say by encouraging quiet members and controlling dominant members.
- Deliberately design small group exercises to encourage parents to work together with *all* other parents in the group.
- Encourage whole group participation and discourage secondary conversations in the group.

A good outline of groupwork strategies and leadership roles is referred to in *A Handbook of Common Groupwork Problems* by Tom Douglas (Routledge, 1991).

Parents' feelings when first attending a group

The lists below are comments made by parents who attended two different fun and families groups in different geographical locations and at different times. The most noticeable feature of the comments is the similarity between them, suggesting a very common set of experiences for parents who are experiencing behaviour difficulties with their children.

Lutterworth: October–December 1991
- I can't cope
- I'm the only one
- My child is a little devil

- I don't know where to turn
- Who can help?
- I'm feeling a failure
- Is it all my fault?
- Where did I go wrong?
- Why me?

Hinckley: February–April 1992

- I am the only one
- Losing my grip
- I hate/have no love for my child
- Couldn't function as a parent
- My child doesn't like me
- Relief if my child is not there
- Beating against a brick wall
- Paranoid
- Dread and fear of the future
- Feel like drink, drugs or escape
- Jealous of other parents
- What am I doing wrong?
- Other people think your children are good.

Part III

The seven-week fun and families programme

7 Understanding behaviour: Sessions 1 and 2

Format of the seven-week programme

The aim of this programme is to present ideas in a practical way, so that they can be tested and practised in carers' own homes for their own use.

Each session is divided into two parts. During the first part the idea of the week is presented. Through discussion and relevant games the theme is demonstrated. In the second half, the group subdivides so that each person can select, and, with help from the others, shape a task to attempt at home. For some this will be more difficult than others; the important thing is to create a manageable but useful task, and often the leader's role is to ensure that something enjoyable is selected. There is a tendency to expect too much of themselves on the part of participants.

It is our practice to make a home visit whenever possible to ensure that people understand what the course entails. Throughout the course these assignments will develop incrementally, so it is very important that they are understood and that a commitment to the whole seven-week programme is encouraged. Participants especially need to understand that practical tasks are an essential part of the work, and that it is not just a discussion group. We encourage them to plan carefully to get the most out of it for themselves by attending every session, but also because others in the group are best supported if a viable number see the programme through.

During the home visit, we ask the parents to fill in a questionnaire. Our own short questionnaire, or the Eyeberg Child Behaviour Inventory, are suitable. Sensitively used, they begin the process of helping participants to feel less alone. The behaviours listed are commonly found in young children, and this often comes as a surprise to parents. The questionnaire is our main measure of progress, and it will be filled in again at the end of the course. Comparisons of behaviour before and after the course can be made and are invariably encouraging.

Other issues can be explored and prepared for. If someone is illiterate they may need a partner to help them, or the course format may need to be adjusted and make less overt use of hand-outs to achieve its end. The need for crèche facilities or transport may be discovered. There may be some cultural issues which they need reassurance about, or the leaders need to do some homework on before the first session. Partners may be persuaded to attend, or at least cooperate more fully than they may otherwise have done. It also provides possibly the only opportunity for the leaders to observe parents and children interacting together.

Finally they are likely to be quite nervous about attending and have a lot of fears or apprehension. In a one-to-one situation it is easier to start reassuring them. Sharing what parents on previous courses have felt and said can be useful in this respect. Our philosophy is that parents are the experts on their own children. With the help they get from the group, they will probably discover which strategies are best for them; they could well be selecting, practising and fine-tuning ideas they are familiar with, rather than learning entirely new tricks.

This part of the book is organised with two main intentions. Each session will be presented in outline. This should provide a checklist for those who are experienced in theory and groupwork. Of course they can amend it to suit their own style and situation but it is useful to have some idea, in this kind of programme, of how much material to include, and the time required to present that effectively without either rushing things or seeming to be too slow. It could be useful to have a copy of this checklist to hand, if and when you are leading a group. A warning would be not to adhere slavishly to the 'programme', but to use it as a prompt. You will then feel more relaxed and be able to create a warm and flexible atmosphere.

The checklist will be elaborated by an expanded presentation of the material included, and comments from our experience about how things have developed in our groups. This is intended for those who are newer to the work – hopefully, it will provide both practical information, but also something of the feel of what happens in groups using this programme.

Session 1: being clear and defining behaviour carefully

Depending upon local circumstances and how well people know each other, a degree of care must be exercised in this introductory session. It may be appropriate to have a warm-up game to introduce them to each other:

Session 1: being clear and defining behaviour carefully

1 Personal introductions

- Warm-up game: Throw the ball and name the person who catches it.
- State the aims of the group. Allow participants to set own ground rules.

2 The main theme: learning to be clear

- Describe difficult behaviours. Put parents' descriptions on flip chart.
- Discuss problems that general or value-laden words produce. Use 'woolly' exercise.
- Practice clear descriptions. Introduce hierarchy model of a tantrum.

3 Tracking behaviour

- The reason for tracking behaviour – Paterson's research.
- The practical use of charts and the rationale.
- The usefulness of monitoring progress.
- Other tracking: diaries, audiotapes, home video, 'typical day' records.

4 Coffee break and socialising

5 Defining behaviour

- Exercise in pairs or in two groups. Work with hand-out and/or own material.

6 Selecting and shaping home task

- Check, in small groups, preciseness of definition.
- Select appropriate tools for each individual.
- Give out charts and folders.
- Offer telephone or referral data for those who might need back-up.

7 Remind people about feedback and importance of trying home tasks.

perhaps throwing a ball round a circle of participators, the receiver shouting out their own name as they catch it, until everyone can remember the other names. That can be tested by changing the rules so that each thrower has to name the person they throw the ball towards.

The important thing is not to go overboard on games and lose the theme of the evening. So try to choose games or exercises which can be fun, but at the same time relate clearly to what is being talked about. You will see that most of the exercises do this.

As part of the preliminaries it can be useful to set out the aims of the group and some of the philosophy behind the programme. In summary, the following may be useful topics to address:

1   Understanding behaviour – The theory behind the group may not be of huge interest to parents: what they will be keen to know is that the course attempts to show how behaviour is influenced and established. Understanding the principles which control behaviour, if they can be explained in plain language, will capture their interest. At its simplest all that needs to be said is that behaviour, generally speaking, is taught. We can therefore teach alternative behaviours if we are dissatisfied with the way our younger children currently behave. It is also possible to discourage, or help unwanted behaviours to be 'unlearned'.

2   Practical alternatives – Above all, the course is about trying out and testing alternative strategies of influencing behaviour. It is not the discussion that is primarily important, but rather the home tasks, and the experience gained in comparing what everyone has discovered there.

3   Positive effectiveness and fun – Our emphasis is always on the positive alternatives. We work hard to generate ways of being with our children which are varied, interesting and fun because we know this works best.

4   Parents are the real experts about their own children – This is because they spend most time with them, and are closest to them emotionally. They will find which things work best, because only they know how their own families operate. All we hope to do through the group is to offer a greater number of ideas, and the means of selecting the best ones, to suit each parent.

5   Confidentiality and informality and sharing (CIS) – In the group we can all learn a lot, and everyone will best contribute to that process if the CIS theme is pursued. We must try to develop trust, friendliness and a genuine sharing, and the leaders' personal experiences should be included in that.

6   Commitment – To the full seven sessions, and to doing the home tasks, and to giving feed-back honestly is important.

7   Ground rules – There will be some things the leaders wish to introduce, but participants also will have items they need reassurance about.

Presenting ground rules successfully is very important but requires sensitivity. In some groups people are very keen to set ground rules; in others they do not really see the need for it. Establishing ground rules can create quite an inhibiting and formal atmosphere if it is not handled well. It may be better to leave it until the second session when people are more comfortable with each other.

Below is one format we have tried.

Group Charter

In any group it helps the smooth running of meetings if everyone can say what their special needs or expectations are. This hand-out provides space to itemise some ground rules. Once they are agreed they can be written down and kept for reference. Others could be added as the group progresses if necessary. It is important that everyone should feel comfortable and this can help. Fun and Families believe it is most important that everyone feels safe to say what they want without fear or favour. Also, in the group, we should avoid using language which could cause offence to other members. We have an anti-discriminatory policy, and although the first eight lines are left for group members to fill in themselves, we have filled in the last two lines because they are items important to us.

1 ....
2 ....
3 ....
4 ....
5 ....
6 ....
7 ....
8 ....
9 We should try to avoid language which may cause offence or show disrespect to another individual's views or customs, whatever their race, creed or sexual orientation.
10 Any personal information shared in these sessions must be treated as strictly confidential and not repeated outside of the group sessions.

The main theme of the evening is helping people to stand back from their situation and learn to describe more clearly the behaviours which irritate or trouble them. One way to start is to ask them to offer one or two descriptions to put on the flip chart. You will get some interesting colloquial descriptions like 'he does me head in' or 'she never stops chelping'. Do not comment at this stage; the idea is to get some fairly general descriptions like 'tantrums' and 'defiance' so that the discussion can be developed. There will probably also be some heavily value-laden and judgmental terms used: she is 'jealous', he is 'aggressive' and so on. Leave these to one side and introduce the 'Woolly' exercise.

'Woolly' exercise

Tick the boxes showing if you think the description in column one is clear and precise, or if it is 'woolly' and unclear and might lead to confusion or misunderstanding.

Description	Tick if 'clear'	Tick if 'woolly'
1 Dinesh is always on the go!		
2 Sally slams the door when she passes through it.		
3 Reena pays attention to requests.		
4 David carries on playing pool after his time.		
5 Anita shows evidence of hyperkinetic syndrome.		
6 Paddy picks his nose.		
7 Sue is immature.		
8 Amrat barges into other kids when asked to line up.		

The 'Woolly' exercise requires individuals to tick columns quickly to indicate whether they believe the descriptions offered are clear or woolly. There is no right or wrong answer – the beauty of this game is that we have never found a group where they were unanimous in their conclusions. A discussion readily grows, or can be prompted when the results are collated. We then ask people to put up their hands if they believe each description is right and collate the numbers on the flip chart. So in a group of ten people the chart may look like this:

Description	Clear	Woolly
1 On the go!	8	2
2 Slams the door	6	4
3 Attention to requests	1	9
4 Playing pool	5	5
5 Hyperkinetic	2	8
6 Picks his nose	9	1
7 Immature	7	3
8 Barges	4	6

The discussion can be developed by asking those who are unclear to put questions to those who were clear about a description which would help clear up their uncertainties. It seems to be particularly important to start by asking those who are unclear to seek more information. If you start with those who are clear the exercise can become quite muddled and unhelpful. Discussions also flow more readily if you focus on those descriptions which found opinions evenly divided. In the figure above this would be questions two and four.

This discussion can be followed by a hand-out to be used in pairs. With this, participants start to practice being more precise. It may seem a little laborious but it is most important to develop this skill of defining. Often people will believe they understand, but when they come to apply it still find themselves struggling. So it is very worthwhile to devise lots of practical tasks to test progress. We often refer to the flip chart and ask if they would like to redefine some of the behaviours they first described. It is

---

Hand-out: defining behaviour

The following three descriptions have elements which are rather vague and general. Try to select the more precise behavioural terms which specifically say *what* the children actually do.

- Sarah is a pain in the neck, she is so defiant. Every time she is asked to do something she screams, shouts and throws her toys across the room. She is so naughty!
- Mira is always demanding and rude. When I have visitors or am doing housework she continually interrupts by shouting, pulling at my dress and being a nuisance!
- Amrat is so 'faddy' with his food. Every time he has to eat, he won't sit still at the table. He shouts and screams and throws his food. He doesn't like anything I give him!

impossible to stress this too much. Later, if a programme is not working well, it will often be found that it was based on a loose definition.

Finally, we break down the description of a tantrum, or defiance, or any chosen behaviour, into its discreet components. We have a hand-out which is designed to introduce the theme: 'One thing leads to another.'

Behaviours can follow a set, almost ritualised, pattern, one thing leading predictably to another. When we think of, and describe, clusters of behaviour individual actions can be missed. More careful observation reveals separate behaviours which we can then arrange in order of severity. This is helpful in selecting the most promising behaviours to try and change.

For example *tantrums* are very commonly viewed as one behaviour. In fact, within a tantrum there are many different behaviours. One three-year-old followed a pattern which regularly progressed from 1) tugging mum's skirt to 2) whining, 3) getting on her knee and blocking eye contact during conversations, 4) jiggling up and down, 5) throwing things about, 6) hitting the baby, 7) crying piercingly, 8) stamping on things and breaking them, 9) holding her breath and finally, 10) head banging.

Mother was understandably most worried about stages 9 and 10. She had scarcely noticed 1 to 3. The following columns help us to see how this happened.

Hand-out: one thing leads to another

1	tugging skirt	A good place to start!	Phase 1
2	whining	These are manageable with firmness or reasoning.	
3	blocking		Phase 2
4	jiggling		
5	throwing	Here, a clash of interests can feel like a wind-up. Mutual agitation makes controlled action difficult.	
6	hitting		
7	crying		
8	stamping		
9	holding breath	Mother can be out of control by this stage.	Phase 3
10	head banging		

In Phase 3, the behaviours have an intense life of their own. They are not open to reason; the child and mother are equally distressed. The point of this analysis and ensuing discussion is to show that often the best place to start, that is, dealing with less difficult behaviours, is overlooked. The more florid behaviours excite our emotions and demand our attention.

The preceding ideas represent a fairly heavy input for most groups. You may well need a break for coffee at this point! You also need to be careful to avoid appearing to lecture. Work at involving the parents in discussion, and slip in reassurances that they know their children best and get them to comment on their own experiences. Emphasise the experimental nature of the sessions, it is essentially about considering ideas then standing back and devising tests to see if and how they are relevant to each individual.

After coffee the task is to find ways to assist parents in standing back and observing what is happening. They need to collect information and order it in a useful fashion. It may be useful to cite the work of people like G.R. Paterson (1974) which indicates that if people can learn to define and track behaviour, the chance to effect change is high. If those skills elude carers the likelihood of getting change is low. Our own experience backs this up, but also demonstrates that the skills are not related to intellect. Some highly educated people find it hard to view things in this very focused way. We have found that less academically able people can sometimes get nearer to objectivity and simply describe what they see and draw eventually useful conclusions from that.

The simplest tool we suggest that might help in tracking behaviour is some form of record chart (see Appendix A). Often parents will be familiar with charts but not fully understand the use to which they can be put. Quite often parents will tell us that they have used charts, and that they were no use. This usually is because programmes have been attempted that are ill thought out and poorly explained, and the use of stars as a reward system has failed. It is worth making the distinction between recording charts and star charts used to change behaviour. Thus discussion offers another opportunity to slip in the need to stand back and not think about change until a better understanding is arrived at upon which to base effective plans.

There are two main tasks related to the use of charts. The first is to have an appreciation of the uses to which they can be put. We use a very obvious fictitious example to promote the debate. Patterns will be quickly seen, but even within those, unjustifiable assumptions will appear. For instance, most assume in the following example that dinnertime is twelve to one. We feel quite self-conscious saying this, but even here, at this stage, people will tend to be jumping to conclusions about problems and remedies. Advise caution; perhaps suggest that twelve to one is worth focusing on for the next week's recording, and even closer assessment. That would make the task easier; it may also reveal that the problem is nothing at all to do with eating. At this point problems could still be redefined, so any solution is premature.

Behaviour record chart

Time	8–9	9–10	10–11	11–12	12–1	1–2	2–3	3–4
Mon			✔		✔✔✔		✔	
Tues	✔	✔	✔		✔✔	✔		✔
Wed			✔		✔✔			
Thurs	✔	✔	✔✔		✔	✔	✔	✔
Fri		✔			✔✔✔		✔	
✔ = Tantrum, i.e., shouting and screaming after being asked to stop								

From this information patterns can be seen: 11 to 12 is always trouble free; tantrums occur all day Thursday; 12 to 1 is a particularly bad time. Now the information could be transposed to a progress chart. In the chart below, the

Progress graph

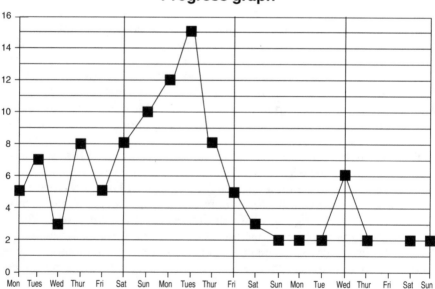

number of tempers per day are simply added together. So the first Thursday shows up as peaking with the highest number of tempers.

On the first Friday we introduced 'time out' to try and reduce the number of tempers. It is quite usual for the behaviour to get worse for a while when attempts to change a behaviour begin. Notice the downward trend from the second Thursday – it is important and offers encouragement. The setback on the third Wednesday is also common and best ignored.

The second task relating to charts is to make sure that each parent has one which relates to their particular needs. It may not be necessary to keep a record for the whole day, but just attend in detail to one hour, or the two or three hours surrounding bedtime. Others may get all they need from a simpler chart like this:

Simplified behaviour record chart

TIME	MORNING	AFTERNOON	EVENING
MON			
TUES			
WED			
THURS			
FRI			

The important things to remember are to keep the task manageable and small enough to be achievable.

Other tracking devices or means of collecting data could be discussed, for example, diaries, especially if people can get quite detailed accounts of particularly trying incidents on a blow-by-blow basis. These accounts should include their feelings as well as the actual events.

Home video- and audio-tapes give incontrovertible evidence from which lessons are often learned without any further help. The audio-tapes can be particularly useful at night with bed-settling routines, as often the actors are too tired to be really calm enough to recall exactly what is happening.

The final section of this session is crucial to the development of the whole course. It involves ensuring that each person goes home with a task they feel comfortable with, and the necessary forms to help them. Enough time should be left in order to allow each person to have an opportunity to make a real selection, and have discussed it with the others. Some will find the work easy, others will need a lot of help if they are to succeed. The most common mistake is to take on too much work, and select too difficult or vague a behaviour to record.

It is our custom to offer telephone contact numbers so that if people do run into difficulty they can get help.

Session 2: putting behaviour into context

Session 2: putting behaviour into context

1   Introductions

- Brief recap on last week
- Feedback on home tasks
  Encourage each parent to contribute in turn, and allow mutual exchange of problems and sucesses.

2   Child development

- 'What is normal behviour?' discussion.
- Use hand-out on childhood norms.
- Discuss gender issues (the different expectations of boys and girls).
- If appropriate, include racial or individual family cultures and religious expectations.

3   The A → B → C model of learning

- Importance of triggers: setting events
- Place of 'pay offs': rewarding consequences

4   Coffee break

5   Exercise 1

'Mr Patel' hand-out: best used in pairs or small groups with feedback to main groups – relate findings to the theory you presented earlier.

6   Exercise 2

View video material – *Kramer v. Kramer* meal time scene is good or use parents' own material. Again relate findings to theory.

7   Divide into small groups to devise home tasks.

This week should begin with a discussion about the recording that was done in the week. That can be used to recap briefly the points made last week. It is important to do this in an informal way, but to keep the links between sessions obvious. Hopefully, and most usually, some in the group will have enjoyed what they did and have discovered for themselves how behaviour 'tracked' in this way is found to follow certain patterns.

Often the behaviour first chosen is not as troublesome or frequent as they thought it to be. The most telling feedback is usually about recording good behaviour. This is a time for genuine sharing and learning, so it is as well not to rush the discussions here, even if there is some straying from the point.

It is again a matter of judging the needs of the group and the time available, but spending time considering 'what is normal behaviour?' can be useful at this point. It provides a chance to discuss gender issues and expectations. The question of labelling children as problems can be dealt with. We often use child development charts to facilitate this debate.

Most important in understanding a child's behaviour is to put that behaviour in context. The ABC model helps us to do this and the main theme of this session is to practice using the ABC formula, the cornerstone of the work. A = Antecedents, that is, events which come before the behaviour. In younger children we look particularly for what comes *immediately* before – seconds rather than minutes – the timing is all important. B = Behaviour which we have selected to observe or change. C = Consequences, that which comes immediately after the behaviour – again, seconds rather than minutes – the timing is all important. There are a number of exercises to be done, and to grasp the application of this model firmly is important and sufficient work for a whole session. Be careful not to overload the input with formal information or peripheral tasks. It may be that you need to come back to spend even more time next week on this subject. There is enough slack in the later stages of the course to permit this. It can hardly be over-emphasised that getting this right is central to the success of the whole programme. If parents grasp this they will take off, and often move well ahead of the leaders in terms of generating their own solutions.

A great deal of research has gone into the ABC model. So that we know that the As and the Cs can determine how well a behaviour is established and maintained.

Behaviours are a response to signals, cues or stimuli. So in looking for the As we discover what it is that provides *prompts* for a behaviour. For example, a 'don't do that' could well prompt and encourage a small child to do something which they may not otherwise have even thought about.

Examples to copy – copycatting or, more technically, modelling – simply describes the way children love to mimic and imitate what they see and hear. If they see mummy putting on make-up they will want to try to do the same! If they hear swearing they will copy that too! If we want a behaviour to occur the best starting point is to *show* the child what we want, which is much more powerful than *telling* them.

Setting events provide opportunities for behaviours to be tried out, and practised. Usually some specific time (bedtime or meal-time), or a particular place (supermarket check-out) or a person (Grandma!) can be identified and associated with troublesome behaviour. Behaviour is more often than not a response to one or more of these features. So if a pattern of behaviour or habits have been formed, changing the As can bring about dramatic changes quite quickly.

Once a behaviour is performed the effect of the consequences (Cs) have an important part to play also. If a behaviour is met with pleasant results, such as lots of attention or praise, it will be reinforced, and the habit will become even more entrenched. Should the Cs be inhibitive, such as ignoring, the behaviour will tend to fade away, and the habit will be broken.

That is the theory. The practice of it, and application to real-life situations is the only way to make it a useful tool for parents. So we have a number of

---

ABC exercise

Select just one behaviour from among many possible behaviours in the following short story. Enter this in the B column. Read the story carefully and fill in the A and C columns with information stated in the story. You do not need to go beyond that material.

Mr Patel takes his five-year-old son shopping, as he does several times a week. In the newsagent's shop Dinesh asks his father for an ice cream. His father has already said 'No' several times. He has already had some sweets, and his father says it is nearly lunchtime. Dinesh starts to whine, then cries lustily; this turns to a scream and he starts to stamp his feet and throw himself about. After five minutes of this, Mr Patel gives in and buys the ice cream. As soon as Dinesh receives it, the crying stops, the tears dry up, and he is quiet and content. Mr Patel feels relieved but impotent.

Antecedent – What happens before	Behaviour – The selected behaviour	Consequences – What happens afterwards

Now discuss what you think is keeping this pattern of behaviours going. Avoid getting caught in how to change things. Concentrate on understanding what is happening to make the behaviour persist.

tasks, which become gradually more difficult and realistic. The first asks the participants, in pairs, to consider the following short story, and to organise the information into the ABC columns.

Remember to give out ABC charts and suggest records be kept. Then, referring to the theory, see if it makes sense, and offers some explanation about how the behaviour is maintained.

The next exercise is a repeat of this but using the information from some video footage. This offers a chance to practice analysing a more life-like situation. There are various teaching materials available, but we have found the sequence from the film *Kramer v Kramer*, where the little boy refused to eat his dinner, to be consistently the most useful and best received material we have found for this purpose.

Discussing the feedback on these exercises is most important, and in doing so try to relate what they notice to the theory. For example, Billy's father constantly says 'Don't you do that!' in the video. That is in effect a prompt or cue which could well encourage that behaviour. Equally the attention it represents could also be rewarding to Billy who desperately wanted his father's attention.

It is important not to rush this process – tease out the meanings, and correct flawed logic or over-interpretation patiently. In some groups people find it almost instinctive to hive away from the model into very elaborate and conjectural hypotheses. It is the leader's task to get them to keep the analysis simple: What comes before? What comes after? How might that influence the behaviour?

The home task is to continue monitoring with the charts, and now build up an ABC analysis around the behaviour they are thinking of trying to change.

8 Influencing behaviour: Sessions 3 and 4

Session 3: encouraging desirable behaviour

This is the week participants long for. They may have anticipated it by trying out their own change strategies, and improvements may have already occurred. One man found that his child stopped crying whenever he went to mark the chart which he had in the kitchen. So without even trying, so to speak, the assessment – standing back and looking – had done all that was needed for him.

Nonetheless, in this session a start is made on planning for change. First of all consider the feedback carefully and try to make explicit links with theory as the parents start to show the triggers and pay-offs that they have discovered. For many, making this conceptual link is difficult. One parent said that since starting the course the behaviour she had chosen, which was fighting, had not been a problem. There were no ABCs to observe therefore. It took quite patient exploration to help her see what had been different in these weeks from previously. Eventually she acknowledged that her custom had been always to wade in angrily to separate her warring offspring. Since the course had begun she had just stood by the door and watched, waiting for the fight to develop and then record it. She was pleased with the change, but it took some time before she could fully appreciate the part her own change in behaviour had played in the improvements.

In this session we hand out our booklet 'Working Together' which provides the simplest outline of the things which can produce change. It was written with the intention that older children could themselves read it, and understand what was being suggested to them.

The emphasis for this week is on starting to work for change by *turning problems on their heads*. We discuss the way that, generally speaking, our

Session 3: encouraging desirable behaviour

1   Recap and feedback

- Warm-up game: say something nice to each other.

2   The most effective means of change

- Be positive; it's more fun and more successful. If one behaviour is encouraged by positive means, others may change with no extra effort.
- So turn the problem on its head.
- Work to increase behaviour you want; stopping what you don't like is examined next week.

3   Encouraging good behaviour

- Give out 'Working Together' booklet.
- Changing the 'As': the triggers.
- Clear messages: sound as if you mean it; use body language that says you mean it.
- Changing the 'Cs': time rewards to match the behaviour you want to increase.
- Discuss the varying effectiveness of different rewards, refer to Step 2a.
- Discuss the difference between bribe and encourager if necessary.

4   Coffee break

5   Stickers and tokens

- Discuss and have stocks available.

6   Exercise

- A small role play to give parents a chance to see how the above skills feel in practice.

7   Devise individual programmes in smaller groups.

8   Home tasks

- Remind about feedback.

thoughts turn instinctively to stopping bad behaviour. That means punishments, and there are many disadvantages in using them. These will be further discussed next week.

Be positive

In this session we seek to practice wherever possible *being positive*. Turning the problem on its head is a helpful way to start. For example, rewarding the child for coming in early rather than having punishments for coming in late is likely to work better. Reward loving statements, rather than try to stop jealous ones; this will create a more productive atmosphere. The reason for this is that:

- It is more enjoyable to administer and to receive positive approaches.
- It has been found in practice more likely that other behaviours will also change, probably because the joy of success encourages other improvements without deliberate work.
- The improvements hold up longer over time.

We ask parents to be clear and single-minded, and select a behaviour they would like to increase. It can be quite telling to ask them to turn the problems they have chosen to work with 'on their heads'. Often a lot of help and puzzling is needed to achieve this. Once again we will be asking that they put to one side issues of punishing and reducing behaviour.

Remember with these methods you can either *increase behaviour(s)* or *decrease behaviour(s)*. It is the simplicity of that approach which gives it success. Be careful not to get sidetracked into looking for more involved explanations. Hold firm to the practical fact that often changing one or two behaviours brings wider benefits.

Use rewards, not punishments

What we want to do is to identify, for each individual, which triggers need to be changed, and which rewards are likely to be effective. We often begin this process with a discussion about rewards and which are the most powerful. Frequently money is seen as top of the list. Indeed that is what children can appear to respond to, and ask for. However, in rank order, hugs and kisses, smiles and encouragement, and genuine attention are most effective. This will sometimes spark a lively debate. In any case, these generalities need refining to individual circumstances, because there will always be the exceptions to rules. Autistic children will probably not respond well to kisses and cuddles, at least at first. Next in descending order are shared activities, games outings, reading together, McDonald's! Money and things rank last on the list, although many parents find this hard to believe.

Another factor in choosing effective rewards is weighing their comparative values for an individual. One young man was very fond of sport, but the chance to learn squash, which he quickly mastered, was not sufficient to outweigh the reward and buzz he got from ruling his mother and sister by bullying. One of the ways of searching for reinforcers which will work is to generate a large list of items which an individual finds attractive. You then have more chance of keeping the programme varied, but also of selecting the most powerful items. We have a questionnaire which many parents find useful, though it is intended only as a guide and should be tailored to individual or family needs. We are very aware that the present format may not accommodate some cultural or class requirements, but the idea of a checklist to help generate ideas can be adapted. This form should be used as a game together, allowing for fantasy and a bit of silliness. Its usefulness is enhanced if it is not treated as a chore or a test. The 'Reinforcement Schedule' is a 4-page, 27-paragraph questionnaire designed to establish individual likes and dislikes. As such it sounds formidable. However, when used as a game played with two participants, rather than as a form to fill in, it has been well received by parents and youngsters who have found it very useful. It provides crucial information to make positive reward strategies work, and to keep them fresh. The 'Reinforcement Schedule' is available from the Centre.

'Adjective spreads' of positive descriptions – qualities each likes to see in others, or themselves – can spur the imagination to consider more positive options. A flip chart will soon be covered with words like 'kind', 'competent', 'helpful', 'musical', 'clever', 'considerate', and others you may never have heard before. This can be used as a variation on the theme of the 'Reinforcement Schedule'. Another idea is to try and record a person pleasing you (or being pleased by you), using a diary or notebook. The list should include some significant actions', phrases or gestures with strong rewarding qualities.

A lot of thought needs to go into devising a plan for change which has a reasonable chance of succeeding first time. It also increases confidence as so many ideas flow and things are noticed which before were being overlooked. It is not enough to recognise that desired behaviour needs encouraging; it is essential to have a customised sense of what will in fact reinforce a behaviour when it occurs.

Preparation for change also frequently necessitates a change in the antecedents. Although it is a rather loose term, parents seem to relate to the idea of triggers. We look for how to trigger off wanted behaviours. Essential ingredients are that clear unequivocal requests be given, which means that attention must be given to language used. Avoid pleading or using phrases that legitimately can be responded to with the answer 'No'. If we say 'Will you please put away your toys?', the child is justified in saying 'No!'. 'It's time to put your toys away now' does not leave room for that, or for a discussion about it!

Looking and sounding as if you mean it is as important as the words. I have seen a mother complain about her child using the most derogatory language, and yet there was a twinkle in her eye, and a tone in her voice which showed how proud she was that he had such spirit. Another parent found she could not simply say 'Time for bed now!' because she believed that it was cruel to demand from a child behaviour which they may not want to do. So she was caught in a trap of needing to *persuade* her child to do anything. The child of course found this a very amusing game. Again you see that in the group it is not enough to list ideas. They have to be thrashed out so that objections or misgivings can be overcome, or suitable strategies for each individual discovered.

Attention is also paid to body posture, and the importance of using eye contact, getting down to the child's level, using touch and judging the right distance to get our message across most effectively. The important thing is to be congruent in the way the message is presented. Strong words and timid retiring body language will only confuse the child.

We find that checklists are useful to make sure nothing is missed; however, overuse of flip charts or overhead projectors can be off-putting and too much like school. Below is one of our checklists which we have on acetate for overhead projectors.

To increase desired behaviour

1 Turn the problem on its head!
  Work to increase a wanted behaviour.

2 Before the behaviour: Antecedents
  Give clear instructions.
  Sound as if you mean it (tone of voice).
  Look as if you mean it (body language).
  Expect success (prepare psychologically and practically).

3 After the behaviour: Consequences
  Use incentives (horses for courses).
  Use token systems.
  Express pleasure and use praise.

4 Before, after and during the behaviour
  Use appropriate body language.
  Be accurate and use appropriate communication.

Another feature, so far not spoken of, has crept into the list above: the use of tokens. Parents and children just love these. What they do is to create the opportunity, in what have often become quite fraught situations, to have a bit of fun. Sometimes it is important to contrive a situation so that something positive can be seen and enjoyed. The purpose of the Fun Stickers is to give additional rewards to children when they behave well. Each time they do so you can encourage them to repeat the behaviour by inviting them to place a sticker on a picture on the inside pages of an album which we have had designed to go with the stickers we produce.

Which behaviours should be rewarded?

If you are trying to reduce a particular unwanted behaviour, such as fighting with brothers or sisters, it is best to use stickers to encourage the opposite behaviour, that is, playing well together or playing without fighting. Guidelines for using the stickers include:

- Give sticker as soon after the behaviour as possible.
- Be clear about why you have given it.
- Do not remove a sticker as a punishment.
- When giving the stickers, use praise and smiles, hugs and cuddles; make it warm and fun.
- Give a sticker every time the behaviour occurs.

The album has been left uncoloured so that children can decorate it themselves, which, if you help them do it, could be an extra incentive. The scene in the album is to allow your children to select where to place the sun, the frog and other stickers, and make more of a game of it.

As a general rule it is most effective to use stickers to reward a behaviour that is an opposite to that which you are trying to reduce. However, if your children do something good there is no harm in giving them an extra sticker. You will find it most effective if you concentrate on one or two specific behaviours, which you feel it necessary to change, at any one time.

Each behaviour we attempt to change is probably either one among a cluster of behaviours, or is set in quite a complex scene. So another principle to attend to is that of breaking things down into small steps. For example, going to bed involves a whole range of activities: putting toys away, washing and getting undressed, goodnight routines and settling down to sleep. Each of these activities can in themselves involve many different behaviours. Putting toys away means picking things up, dropping them into a box, pushing the box into a corner. Getting undressed requires removing many items of clothes, especially in the winter. Each item removed requires complex manual and physical skill. Though this may seem as if we are going into unnecessary detail, you will find that attempts to change a behaviour will be much more successful if you select a small and precise task. When that is achieved other items can be added. This is called 'shaping'. Putting toys away could start just with picking things up, and rewarding that. Then gradually add the actual putting-away of the toys. Sometimes the other stages then follow without further effort and then great encouragement is gained.

If this process of breaking down complex tasks is overlooked it is far more likely that too large a task will be selected and the efforts to change will be thwarted. It is discouraging then to have to go back to square one.

Once all these principles have been aired, we must put flesh on the bones, so to speak, and get the group to practise putting all the different components together. Parents say they learn most from role plays. Our experience is that many professionals and group leaders become very anxious about this. It could be that they expect too much from it, or feel overwhelmed that some emotional experiences will develop which are beyond their ability to deal with. We have found a very simple formula that works well and is fun, and has so far never got out of hand. What we do really is to ham it up and go right over the top.

Our first step is to enact a scene, say, putting toys away, but for the parent to do it very badly indeed. Usually one of us will go outside the room and simply shout, rather rudely, through the door for the toys to be tidied away. The person playing the child of course takes no notice. Parents are then invited to criticise the performance, which they can easily do.

Most importantly, when someone offers a criticism, we ask them to not just say how it should be done, but to show us how they could improve on it themselves. In this way the whole group can become involved in having a lot of fun, but at the same time practising what for some of them may be quite new and tricky skills. One mother confessed she had never really cuddled her little girl or put her arms round her much. She found it very difficult to do at first, but once she began to try, it rapidly became a pleasure for her.

We have a checklist for parents so that essential components can be ticked off as they are included in the attempt to get the child to conform.

As a teaching device, we ask parents to include all the components on the list, even though that is a little artificial. The checklist includes the following:

- Body: Assume a confident posture – look as if you mean business. Get close to the child; make and maintain eye contact and use touch.
- Verbal: Avoid questions or pleading, be firm. Expect the response you want.
- Context: Be reasonable and give time for a response. Offer incentives.

- Give praise: Use stickers and make a game of it.
- Express *genuine* feelings: 'Mummy will be pleased', 'Mummy is tired and angry'. (This use of emotion can cause a great deal of trouble, and needs careful preparation and practice.)

Gradually, everyone is encouraged to shape up and improve on their performance.

Remember the course is not primarily about discussing things; it is essentially a task-centred course, in which practice enables parents to try out new things, and to refine their own strategies. In the group, we model and shape up behaviours so that the parents increase their confidence. Then at home they will model for their children behaviours which they wish to encourage, and instinctively try things which discussion alone would not inspire them to do.

After coffee (which you will probably need), divide into smaller groups and agree upon home tasks for each participant. Encourage everyone to keep the recording going, and to use the booklet 'Working Together' as a reference.

Session 4: discouraging unwanted behaviour

In theoretical terms the definition of 'punishment' is any action which reduces the frequency of a behaviour. It is an undesirable behaviour that is punished, *not* the child. This is a subtle but important point, particularly when the discussions move round to questioning why should we avoid punishing a naughty child, or what is the purpose of rewarding a naughty child. We are not rewarding the child, but an alternative behaviour!

There are numerous strategies for discouraging unwanted behaviour *but* they all have drawbacks when used. They are less than pleasant to administer, and equally aversive to receive. It follows then that there is quite a high risk that relationships will be damaged and feelings hurt in the process, so a discussion about this is important. Often thinking about changing behaviour begins with 'How can I stop this?' and then 'What punishments will work?' It appears to be almost instinctive to believe that physical pain is a deterrent.

Smacking or hitting embraces all the disadvantages of punishing techniques in their most exaggerated form. The trap is sprung when a punishment is first administered, because it *does* appear to work. A child will stop whingeing if smacked (though they may start screaming instead!), but only for a while. The next time the smack will be less effective, and thus a parent can find themselves smacking more and more, or harder and harder. Parents in our groups acknowledge again and again that smacking does not

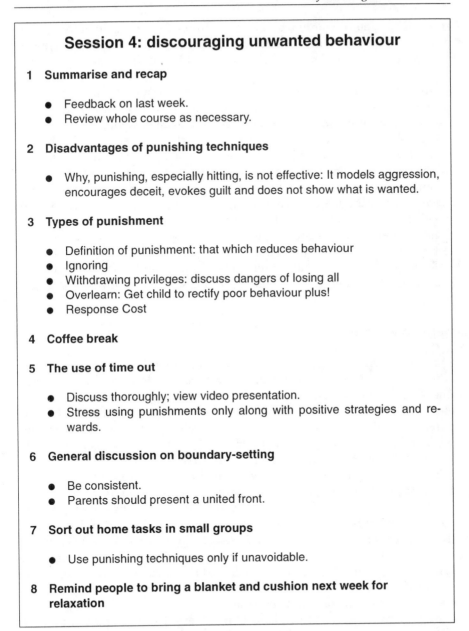

Session 4: discouraging unwanted behaviour

1 Summarise and recap

- Feedback on last week.
- Review whole course as necessary.

2 Disadvantages of punishing techniques

- Why, punishing, especially hitting, is not effective: It models aggression, encourages deceit, evokes guilt and does not show what is wanted.

3 Types of punishment

- Definition of punishment: that which reduces behaviour
- Ignoring
- Withdrawing privileges: discuss dangers of losing all
- Overlearn: Get child to rectify poor behaviour plus!
- Response Cost

4 Coffee break

5 The use of time out

- Discuss thoroughly; view video presentation.
- Stress using punishments only along with positive strategies and rewards.

6 General discussion on boundary-setting

- Be consistent.
- Parents should present a united front.

7 Sort out home tasks in small groups

- Use punishing techniques only if unavoidable.

8 Remind people to bring a blanket and cushion next week for relaxation

work, but if they have no other strategies they will do it out of frustration. Smacking gives them momentary relief but then leaves them feeling guilty. Quite often this leads to a cuddle, and attempts to undo the hurt. By this time the child is swamped with mixed, unclear messages, but knows that after all he gets rewarded by close attention for doing something, that provoked a hit in the first instance. If a child gets little attention as a general rule, a smack can be rewarding in itself, as it is powerful emotional attention.

Another disadvantage is that punishment techniques do not say what is wanted. Unless combined carefully with the positive strategies, there is a vacuum of information, and a no-win situation can develop.

Most significant and worrying is the research which shows what hitting in fact teaches. It first of all models violence as a legitimate way of influencing people. Children learn, through being hit, that it is an acceptable way to try and make people do as you want. G. R. Paterson's research (1994) testifies that where there is excessive hitting in childhood, criminality frequently develops as the child grows older. Besides teaching violence as a means of social influence, it also encourages deceitfulness. The lesson of violence is not 'Don't do that again' but '*Do not get caught* doing it.'

There is a huge potential for misunderstanding and frustration in using punishing techniques, and therefore a full discussion follows on different types of punishment.

Selective ignoring

Selective ignoring simply means withdrawing attention when a behaviour is targeted for reduction. For example, a young child swears in company. The shocked horror and 'don't be naughty' protests put the child immediately centre stage. Such attention is most encouraging despite what the parent's words are saying – the child may well repeat it just for effect, and work it up into an exciting game. However, if the bad words are totally ignored it is unlikely that they will be repeated.

This very simple principle can be applied to quite severe situations. One boy constantly absconded from residential school, and from the courts when he was arraigned for offences. He was surrounded by escorts, and the moment he got back to school he would run again, in the full knowledge that a team and the police would be searching for him. A very brave management decision was made: to not go after him, or report him. He turned up at court of his own free will, and made his own way back to the school afterwards. Quite a high degree of nerve and belief in the principles are needed to enact something like that.

Besides trusting the principle, it is necessary also to implement it in a technically correct way. A degree of dramatisation is sometimes needed. Ignoring is not a passive thing – it is an active demonstration that no interest or reinforcement will accompany unwanted behaviours. It can be worth practising how to plan and use it. First, the right words are needed: perhaps something like 'You are being silly now, I'll not watch' would be a suitable signal, to make clear that the behaviour was unacceptable. Then decide how to back that up with action. Deliberately turning away, or leaving the room might be necessary. It is not sufficient to say something if your actions show you are still amused. Children are very clever at catching our eye, making a joke of something, and melting our resolve. So ignoring needs to be planned, and the child needs to know what is going to happen before the event.

Withdrawing privileges

Most people will be well aware of the effectiveness of refusing a child a favourite TV programme. However, the discussion of withdrawing privileges must go beyond a list of things which might be withdrawn. It will be more helpful for carers to understand some of the reasons why removing privileges sometimes does not seem to work.

Just as thinking about what might be most rewarding to individual young people, and weighing carefully which reinforcements will be strongest to them, is important, so also is the comparative significance of withdrawing things. Parents quite often misjudge the value a child puts on particular things, and may be quite surprised at the apparent ease with which the child discounts it, and takes little notice of the deprivation.

Another feature that prevents this strategy working is if it cannot be implemented. The classic 'Right, you are grounded for a *month*' would only in exceptional homes be possible to stick to for either the parent or the child.

Not only must the punishment be possible to administer, it should also be fair! It can be very useful to involve the young person in deciding which thing they should lose. Older children are usually much more severe on themselves than we would be. So a very workable compromise can be reached if you end up agreeing to remove less than the youngster themselves thought would be appropriate.

A major pitfall will arise if the ground rules are not strictly adhered to. Privileges should only be withdrawn for specific, pre-defined misbehaviour. It can be very tempting to take something away if a new aggravation emerges. The effectiveness of the strategies will diminish if they are used too generally and broadly without careful thought and preparation.

Response cost programmes

'Response cost' programmes are a way of ensuring that withdrawing privileges is set up fairly, kept within a positive framework, and administered effectively. The response cost programme is really a combination of techniques both positive and punitive. It is intended to demonstrate that a child's individual actions can have consequences, which are within their own control. Thus, they can, in effect, earn rewards or incur costs to themselves.

The programme uses negotiation skills, positive encouragements, social praise, and hugs, for example, but also the removal of privileges when identified unacceptable behaviour occurs. Below is one way it could be arranged.

- Use a small notebook. Keep this where the child can readily see it and look at it to check progress.
- Keep the first few pages to write down the rules or agreements you make, and the subsequent changes to them. For example, the first page may look like this:

Agreement
1. *Every time I washes the dishes, or puts the rubbish in the dustbin he will receive a token of his own choice.*
2. *These will be given as near to the event as possible, and be accompanied with praise and encouragement as the token is put in the book.*
3. *Such tokens will not in any circumstances be taken away.*
4. *It will be possible to earn 14 tokens each week (2 per day). These may be exchanged for items included in the menu.*

- A menu can be written at the back of the book. It is generated as a fantasy game. The child can put down, or ask for anything they want to be included, no matter what the cost or practicalities. In order to keep control of this situation, the parent allocates the number of tokens needed to acquire each item. The menu can be added to at any time. It may look something like this:

Trip to the cinema	10	*Reggae Cd*	100	*McDonald's*	3
Disco	50	*Trip to Disneyland*	2,000,000	*Late TV*	75
Theme Park	400	*Mountain Bike*	10,000		
New Trainers	150				

- It might be helpful to rule the middle pages of the book so that the tokens could be fixed there, and at the same time an overview of progress be created.
- You will notice in the following example that a column has been allowed for bonuses. Perhaps you could offer 5 bonus points for every 6 normal points earned, which would increase the weekly total to a possible 24. Notice the scheme offers incentive for partial success. Six points is less than half-way home, it is wise to build in allowance for some slippage of performance.

- So the page might look like this:

	Washing Up	Rubbish Out	Bonus
brought forward			
Monday			
Tuesday			
Wednesday			
Thursday			
Friday			
Saturday			
Sunday			
TOTALS			
Total carried forward less trade-ins and penalties			

- The cost element in this case would be to remove bonus points only. The child must never lose everything. So the ground rules may include a sentence such as 'Every time J hits Y two bonus points will be deducted'.
- The tokens could be similar to the stickers spoken of earlier in this chapter (see p. 90), or you could simply mark the book, or use stars or other simple symbols such as coloured dots.

There would be many variants on these themes depending upon the age of the child, and their particular interests. More visible token schemes could be devised – dropping marbles into a transparent tube, collecting 1p's in a bottle. 'Worms in a box!' were suggested by one mum whose little boy was fascinated with worms. Keep it fresh, fair, and flexible, and the most important thing is to make the whole thing a game and keep it fun!

Overlearning

When a child is asked to do something but refuses, and it is absolutely clear that the refusal is about avoiding to comply, a technique called 'overlearning' can be effective. It is probably more appropriate for older toddlers and adolescents. Overlearning involves getting them to comply and do the task requested, but do a bit more as well. For example, if they are asked to put their toys in the box but refuse, then they must be made to do it, without help, and not only put the toys in the box, but also put the box away.

This is not easy advice and could well involve some resistance and the need for being very firm and persuasive indeed. However the task in the short term is to demonstrate that avoiding requests is not worthwhile.

Time out

'Time out' is a very effective means of preventing attention-seeking behaviour from getting out of hand and teaching habits which could be detrimental to the child's future. In the section above, on overlearning, we refer to what sense a behaviour has for the child, as well as the actual behaviour. Refusing to put toys in the box could equally be the child trying to gain attention, as well as to avoid tidying up. If the child becomes centre stage and has an audience, that in itself could be reason enough to make a game of delay, in order to enjoy the attention, even if that attention was becoming rather agitated.

There is a need to select these techniques with some care, otherwise you will get a sneaking feeling that things are not working, or that you are making things more difficult for yourself.

Time out is frequently used: parents send their children to sit at the bottom of the stairs, or stand in a corner until they are calm. In some ways, it is not so much a punishment as a means of teaching the child how to control outbursts of temper, or showing-off, which goes too far. Unfortunately, variants of time out can be abusive. For example, to shut a child in its bedroom for hours is not really time out, and yet it is mistaken for that.

In this session we usually show some video footage of time out being practised. The material is then discussed. The discussion is important because there are many variations on the theme, and individual circumstances demand different detail. The places available to move the child to, for example, may be limited. Depending upon the history of the behaviour and the parent's previous attempts to curtail it, it might be better for the parent to remove themselves rather than attempt to move the child.

Of all the issues covered in the course, time out is the one which most frequently polarises members. They either say it is great, or that it is horrible and they would never use it. However, for those who are comfortable with it, it is very effective *but* must be got right from the time it is first used. Usually the lesson is quickly learned and the behaviour should improve in a matter of days.

When first using time out, it is possible that the child will respond with an increase in angry or violent responses for a short period of time. The first time it is used we have known it to take an hour or more for the child to settle down. This is obviously a very harrowing experience for parents. Indeed, in some cases, matters have got out of hand. If time out is attempted and then abandoned before the procedure is completed the behaviour is likely to become even more entrenched, and the parent more despairing. So it needs to be well planned, and possibly the parent should have help or support when first implementing it. Time out works in a number of stages:

- The procedure involves first telling the child what to expect when next they behave in the difficult manner.
- When the behaviour occurs, warn them that time out will be used.
- If they do not comply, repeat the warning.
- Do not repeat it a third time, but take the child to the time-out place. It's best to hold them from behind and avoid eye contact. It must be a firm, unemotional action.
- S/he must stay there until they have been quiet for about three minutes (certainly no more than five minutes).

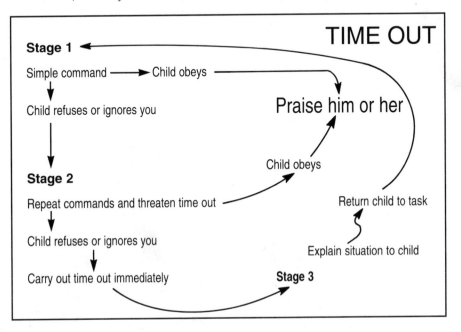

- The parent should then go and quietly praise them for calming down and being quiet, and bring them back to the play area. (It is important that the return to their activities is initiated by the parents, and not at the demand of the child.)
- If they start to play up again, then repeat the procedure.

References for this procedure can be found in Martin Herbert (1987). We have some video material which depicts how *not* to use time out, which is useful for discussion. Sometimes, we find people learn more from criticising bad performances, than accepting very good ones without question. Currently in the groups we use the video *Breaking in Children* but do not like the name or some of the details it depicts. However, it always promotes a good discussion and outlines the essential points.

We always stress that these techniques should always be used in combination with rewarding strategies, and always kept as a last resort.

Some parents experience considerable difficulty in establishing boundaries. Again, discussion regarding family rules, and the security children find in knowing where they stand is worthwhile.

The last part of the session allows time for each parent to shape up their home task for the week. Many by this stage will have a plan in operation and will not need to use the punitive strategies. It is important to encourage them in what they are doing by continued interest and exchanging feedback from their efforts.

At the end of the session, refer to next week's activities as they may like to wear casual clothes and bring a pillow and blanket with them for the relaxation exercise.

9 Stress management and self-evaluation: Sessions 5, 6 and 7

Session 5: looking after ourselves

Session 5: looking after ourselves

1 Recap on last week

- Discuss progress and individual programmes.

2 Parents' thoughts and feelings; dealing with stress

- Unhelpful thoughts and beliefs can affect feelings, behaviour and coping capacities.

3 Flip chart exercise

- Examine beliefs, thoughts and feelings about parental abilities.
- How group members felt at the beginning of Group.
- Compare with other parents from previous Groups.

4 External pressures

- Society and culture, expectations, myths.
- Family and friends: advice, etc.
- Children objectified: 'little devils', etc.

5 The A $\rightarrow$ B $\rightarrow$ C $\rightarrow$ O model

- Emphasising the B $\rightarrow$ C link. *continued*

- Alternative beliefs.
- Challenges and disputes; coping statements; distractions.
- Give out exercise sheets – do exercise singly or in pairs.

6 Coffee break

7 Relaxation as a coping mechanism

- Relaxation increases coping abilities, e.g. anger control.
- Demonstrate signs of stress and tension, e.g. clenching fists, gritting teeth.
- Discuss positives of recognising when under stress; aim to identify stress 'triggers'.
- Link anger control to the use of coping statements.

8 Relaxation exercise – all do together!

9 Parents' future plans

- What are parents' ideas, feelings about future?
- Mention parents' support groups.
- What will the group do in Sessions 6 and 7?

10 Home tasks

- Use coping statements at home.

By this stage in the course the feedback should flow quite readily, and so it is important to allow sufficient time – at least 20 minutes – for parents to share their personal thoughts and feelings. We find that parents are by this time recapping and fine-tuning their work, and some may even be at the point of wanting the discussions to range over a wider field of topics.

In this session there is opportunity to use your own particular skills and local knowledge to create links for the future or to wind down the group to finish on a constructive note. Many participants feel almost bereft, if the group has gone well, at the prospect of it finishing. You may not want to use the particular format we do. It may be that you select only parts which you feel competent and comfortable with.

We use this session to present a model which can be helpful in shaping behaviour. By way of introduction this little illustration can be used:

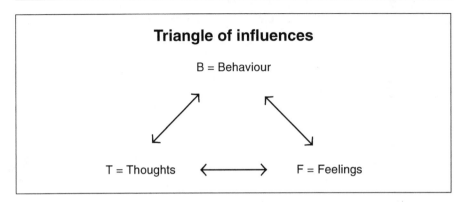

We then suggest that the work we have done has focused quite specifically on changing behaviour. This was because the techniques are well tried and that this is probably the easiest thing to achieve.

Dealing with stress: changing the way we think

Problems can be manifest in other ways even though they are closely linked. Behaviour is very directly influenced by what we feel: if we are feeling ill, or angry, or profoundly sad, it is difficult to get on with work, or react socially as we normally would. We may behave untypically and sometimes be immobilised until we have regained our composure. What we want to consider is how much control we can develop in regard to our feelings. To finish the session we practise some simple relaxation techniques to illustrate what can be done to improve our control.

Thinking also can affect the way we behave, and the way we feel. Chapter 5 sets out in some detail the principles of cognitive behavioural theory. What we try to do is to provide parents with a simple but useful acquaintance with those ideas which illustrate the powerful influence that thinking can have over both behaviour and feelings.

All we do in this session is use the grid from Chapter 5 to encourage discussion and to play about with, perhaps including examples personal to ourselves or group members if that seems appropriate. The process could develop sequentially as follows:

1   Think of an event that is commonly most stressful to you and put it in the first column.

Event	thought	feeling	outcome
a temper tantrum			

2   Now try to recall how such an event makes you feel!

Event	thought	feeling	outcome
a temper tantrum		*helpless*	

3   What story might you have been telling yourself as this was going on?

Event	thought	feeling	outcome
a temper tantrum	*I can't control my child*	*helpless*	

4   Can we predict what the outcome might be? A possibility would be:

Event	thought	feeling	outcome
a temper tantrum	*I can't control my child*	*helpless*	*do nothing*

Most will be able to identify with something like this, or produce their own particular scenario which commonly troubles them. The usefulness of this can be explained. Just as we spent some time identifying and defining carefully which child behaviours were troublesome, and made this the starting point to change things, so we can change thinking by identifying which stories we tell ourselves that habitually are unhelpful. Previously, we've looked for behaviour patterns to change during the course, in this case we look for thought patterns to change.

Now if the table at Step 4 makes sense but is seen to be unhelpful, you can move on to generate alternatives:

5 Identify what might be a more positive thing to tell yourself – or can you think of someone else who would tell themselves something quite different? Put that in the second row of the table.

Event	thought	feeling	outcome
a temper tantrum	I can't control my child	helpless	do nothing
	I won't put up with this		

6 Such a thought creates an entirely different feeling, instead of feeling helpless, it stirs the adrenaline and ideas and promotes activity. The result could then be:

Event	thought	feeling	outcome
a temper tantrum	I can't control my child	helpless	do nothing
	I won't put up with this	determined...angry	use time out?

It is worth working through several examples, and dealing with the questions which arise.

Quite often this is where the idea of follow-up courses or support groups can be promoted. Clearly, this is only a taster of using this model to full advantage and some may well be keen to learn more. They may want books, or information about evening classes, or they may ask you to help them arrange some instruction for an extended or completely new group. This discussion should take you through to coffee-break time.

Dealing with stress: relaxation techniques

After coffee, we talk briefly about how individuals cope with stress. Sometimes a member of the group is present who does yoga, or something similar, who could introduce or lead the relaxation. It is best to have completed all the work of the evening before starting the relaxation, so that people can go home feeling the most benefit from just winding down in that way. Make sure all notices or reminders have been given before this point.

We have a tape available if you are not confident enough, at first, to lead the exercise yourself. The point we want to make is that, with practice, we can all learn to have some control and quite quickly alleviate the worst effects of anxiety and stress as they occur.

The relaxation exercises on the tape we have produced includes examples of various techniques.

In the session we offer only a taste of a small range of relaxation techniques. This is done by using a sequence which includes muscle relaxation, deep breathing and meditation. Any of these could be taken to much higher levels of expertise than we have time for in the group session. The idea is to provide a choice, so that participants can select what will individually suit them best.

The tape dwells on the theme of sand and beaches. Obviously this will not suit everybody. However, there are various other themes such as water, wind, music, bird-song, and all are available on commercial tapes.

Here is an excerpt from our tape:

Before you begin it is important that you're comfortable. So perhaps just stretch out your legs in front of you – wiggle yourself into a comfortable position on your chair, or if you prefer, lie stretched out on the floor. After this brief practice you should not feel you have to rush away to the next task, so once the talking stops, allow yourself to come back into the room and to the other people, in your own time, no matter what others may be doing.

Now, first of all we will practise realising the level of control we can have over our own bodies, and the tension that develops in it from time to time.

To do this, I would like you to hold an arm out in front of you. Then clench your fist as tightly as you can, making the finger nails dig into the palm. At the same time, push the arm forward, feeling it stretch and strain and quiver.

Now... let it go! Let your arm rest limply on your lap or by your side, and tease out the fingers, wriggling and loosening them. And feel the difference! Register the difference! And realise that, when we get anxious, our bodies tense up like that, but also realise that if we are aware of it, we can, with practice, let go.

Try just one more exercise.

This time tighten up your face, clench your teeth, press them together really hard so that you feel the muscles of your jaw strain. Screw up your eyes so that you furrow your forehead into a tight frown, straining the muscles round the forehead and cheeks almost to aching point. And now... let it go!

Shake your head...

Soften your eyes...

If you can, let your forehead relax.

It may not be possible, but nonetheless, feel the difference, your face more relaxed and comfortable. Make sure that your teeth are not together but slightly apart; your lips also could be slightly open. Notice how your breath moves, naturally, quietly, just as your body wants it to. Notice the difference!

We will move on now to concentrate a little more specifically on our breathing.

What I would like you to do is to notice the tip of your nose, just concentrate on the tip of your nose. When you breathe in, notice the air passing through your nose:

IN (breathe deeply)   OUT (exhale firmly)
IN   OUT

Just notice the air coming in from the outside filling your body with life and energy and peace. Then lay back so that you are one with the life around and in you. Notice the breathing, and be aware of it going

IN   OUT

It doesn't matter if your mind wanders, but try to keep bringing it back to the breathing and letting the air course in and out, slowly, slowly caressing your nose! You will notice you relax more and more:

IN (deep breath in)   OUT (firmly exhale)
IN   OUT

Now to build up a scene in your imagination, marry this IN and OUT of the air passing your nose to the tide lapping gently IN and OUT on a beach of soft golden sand. Spread your towel on the sand, and put down any packs; take off any tight clothes. Lie down and feel the weight of your body being carried by the sand, sand that shifts, as you wriggle, to make a comfortable custom-made bed.

You are relaxing, feeling your arms resting on the sand, and your fingers playing with the soft tickling sand. Your back is supported and comfortable, your chest rises and falls … slowly, and yet more slowly. Your eyes become softer, heavier and softer, and still the air is coursing past the tip of your nose with great IN (suck in a breath)

and OUT (push out a breath)
so slowly IN and OUT.

All of this links with the rhythm of the sea, still gently lapping, you notice your bottom comfortably supported but wriggle to make it even more so, more and more comfortable. Your thighs and calves are supported by the sand.

You raise one leg. Then feel your foot push into the sand caressing the soft silky grains. You and your body are one with the world around you, this beautiful, warm, encouraging, restful world.

Still your breathing gets slower and calmer and your nose notices everything! as the air comes IN and OUT.

You hear the surf, scent the hibiscus at the beach's edge, you sense and see, in your mind's eye, the soft rustling of the palms there. Your body feels heavier and heavier pressing snugly into the sand. With your own rhythm, settle down and relish all this (you don't need my words now) let your own imagination catch everything that comes in on your breath

IN through your nose
OUT through your nose

quietly … restfully … blissfully …

Without knowing it, you are charging your batteries – quietly the energy of the sea, and the wind and your heart is filling you, replenishing you, to make you fresh and full of energy and peace and hope …

I will stop talking and let you decide when, in your own time, to return to this room and this company.

The group then breaks up in its own time to say farewells or simply disperse.

Session 6: evaluating progress

Session 6: evaluating progress

- Feedback from week and using coping statements.
- Troubleshooting.
- Use to complete information not yet covered.
- Discuss plans for the future (i.e., parents' support group and timing of the Seventh Session).
- Complete evaluation forms so that parents can see the progress they have made. It is useful to return the original evaluation form at this point as a means of comparison.

It can be quite useful to put on a flip chart, or collect in some way, the comments made at this session. Apart from the encouragement it provides parents, the comments can be used to demonstrate the success of your own work. Perhaps it will provide data to encourage members of future groups, if you set up a rolling programme. It can also be evidence, or at least offer indicators that you have achieved change. This can be important in terms of getting continued funding and management approval.

During the troubleshooting period there may emerge some parents who clearly still have further work to do, and who need ongoing support. You have either therefore to mobilise this from within your own resources or perhaps refer them on. We have found locally that Home Start can often provide valuable support.

Throughout the programme we find that it is best to give a very high priority to the theme of the week. There is more than enough material to absorb if that is dealt with thoroughly. However, people inevitably work at different paces and so some will appreciate more information. Some of this could be included in this session. One group asked if we had readily available a list of references so that certain areas could be examined in more depth. In response to that we are producing a parent's manual, intended to complement the programme but also to be useful in its own right to carers who have no access to groups.

Plan the seventh session. Often this is simply a social occasion, providing an opportunity for people to mark the end of the group. The most successful ideas will come from parents themselves and they will offer the most practical and apposite suggestions for their own locality. It is worth taking the time, and resisting the temptation to offer your own ideas, in order to encourage them to speak.

This session includes filling in another questionnaire, which then can provide a 'before' and 'after' profile. It would be helpful to make an anonymous graph of this data. Clearly if one member was struggling and the results would be an embarrassment to them it would be best not to use it immediately. But for future groups and home visits such visual evidence is easily understood and gives powerful encouraging messages. Remember to collect and feedback to participants as many different indicators of success as possible. Some groups will not object to the use of video recordings, and these could be used to make comparisons with where people were and now find themselves. Anecdotal material (Mrs X said she had seen you looking so much better!), and just simple but accurate observations can all enhance the sense of achievement and well-being which is what we hope to achieve.

On this occasion people are encouraged to keep their records and efforts going, to see how it feels to work without the support of the group. The seventh session is planned three weeks to a month ahead to allow some 'solo' activity to take place, while the safety net of at least one more session is available. Any final troubleshooting or referrals can be discussed and organised informally within that context.

Session 7: troubleshooting and planning future support

Session 7: troubleshooting and planning future support

- This is usually arranged three weeks later in order to allow parents the chance to practise their new-found skills at home and to make sure that unwanted behaviours do not return.
- It can be linked to a social event, perhaps a trip to the pub, going out for a meal, or a bring-your-own buffet, etc.

It is not very easy to write about this session, as it needs to be the participants' own evening. The content or agendas will therefore vary widely. The main purpose of the evening is to create an informal, relaxed and socially entertaining evening. Some will use this to discuss their progress with managing behaviours, but others will have already moved on to considering other issues, or perhaps just be there for a good night out.

The essence of an effective support group is that parents should want to arrange it and run it for themselves. One recent group took this to the extent of arranging a support group and deliberately not inviting the group leaders. Whilst the leaders felt initially a little shocked, they recognised that the parents meeting and organising the group alone was the most effective and ideal way for a support group to run.

So Session 7 works best when the leaders let go, and the parents plan for their own future support. Chapter 12 offers more detail about setting up support groups, but Session 7 is a good time to encourage their formation.

In Birkenhead, leaders and parents combined and ran an additional course called 'Feeling Good', when the Fun and Families group had finished. The programme included:

Week 1   Being me ... being a parent ... our dreams
    2   Motherhood ... how it used to be ... how it is now
    3   Stress and how to cope with it
    4   Confidence and what to do with it
    5   Sex ... relationships ... you can choose
    6   Physical pleasure ... aromatherapy
    7   How we are feeling now ... evaluation

This was so successful that they ran another course called 'Staying Feeling Good'. Details about this innovative work can be obtained from Julie Cookson, Beechcroft House, Whetstone Lane, Birkenhead, Wirral L41 2SN, phone 0151 650 1970, or Sheila Hughes, Fender Primary School, New Hey Road, Woodchurch, Wirral L49 8HB, phone 0151 604 1208.

One of the most memorable evenings involved exploring play. Everyone was asked to list the things they had done to amuse themselves when they were young children. They were then encouraged to actually play some of those games together. Besides being a hilarious trip down memory lane, it also released all manner of inhibitions, and enabled us all to think much more imaginatively about how to divert or influence young children towards things they might genuinely enjoy. We now use this theme in training group leaders, and it is always well received.

Week seven should be a relaxed and a fun-filled evening, a chance to say goodbyes, but also to create opportunities to be looked forward to.

Part IV

Evaluation and parents' support groups

10 Evaluation

How to evaluate: measures and indicators

Why is it important to evaluate?

For many practitioners the idea of evaluation can be both threatening and time-consuming. The Centre believes evaluation to be both positive and constructive. The following points argue strongly that, with minimum effort, evaluation can be both time- and cost-effective.

- Evaluation means gathering information, data or evidence which can be used to measure effectiveness. It can also have applications in the setting of standards and gives the 'user' an opportunity to have a say about the quality of service.
- Evaluation is about partnership and co-operation between clients and practitioners. It is a dynamic and ongoing process in which many lessons can be learned about needs and appropriate responses.
- We cannot assume that intervention has been effective, either with individual casework or groupwork. Therefore, success or failure can only be gauged if clear measures are established beforehand.
- Good planning, whereby clear goals and targets are negotiated, facilitates evaluation and saves time in the long run.
- Evaluation must play a crucial role in meeting the objectives of the Children Act and establishing good working practices.
- Evaluation increases effectiveness and the quality of practice because it provides both the evidence for success and the reasons why interventions can go wrong.
- Clients should expect and deserve an effective evaluated service which meets their needs.

- Evaluation gives clear evidence to higher management that using these behavioural approaches in a thorough and effective manner does show extremely good research-based results. This evidence is very cost-effective in the long run.

The evaluation process

The following flow chart or model illustrates the Centre's groupwork approach with parents and demonstrates the dynamic and fluid nature of the evaluation process. Measuring effectiveness is not always the final stage as it can lead to renegotiation of objectives. In the evaluation process partnership, negotiation and client involvement are central elements, in just the same way as they are crucial when working within the spirit of the Children Act (1989).

The evaluation process

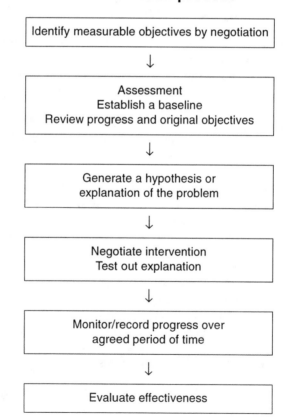

How should I evaluate?

In setting up and running a group, or carrying out individual work, it is important to take a 'nuts and bolts' approach, that is, decide what you are measuring and why you are doing so. In our groupwork programme for parents of children aged one to eleven years, there are a number of measurable elements:

- Frequency and number of child behaviour difficulties reported by parents
- Parental satisfaction with each session and progress as a whole
- Parental reported improvement and progress in the 'target' behaviours
- Parental thoughts, feelings and beliefs (primarily for research study purposes)
- Parent-child interaction within the natural home environment (primarily for research study purposes).

How to measure

The following seven measuring devices have been used in our groupwork programmes.

Child Behaviour Inventory   Approximately three weeks before the beginning of the groupwork programme, all the parents are visited at home. They are asked to complete a child questionnaire which is based on the Eyeberg Child Behaviour Inventory (see Appendix B, p. 142). This is designed to measure the frequency and number of child behaviour problems. It provides valuable baseline or assessment data which gives a benchmark to measure change. Central areas include views on punishment, discipline, explanations for behaviour problems and experience of parenthood. The questionnaire has proved useful in child protection or risk assessment work as it can reveal potential stress indicators. Male or female partners are asked to complete the questionnaire independently. This can often illustrate large discrepancies between the partners.

During Session 6, parents reflect on the programme as a whole. They again complete the same questionnaire as they did in Session 1, and the two papers are compared in order to find out if change has occurred. The aim is to assess parents' reported changes in their children's behaviour problems from the beginning to the end of the course. The final session is then held three weeks later in order to 'troubleshoot' any likely problems and to assess if progress has been maintained over a greater length of time.

Tracking and recording   The first two sessions aim to equip parents with the necessary skills to systematically define, track and record child behaviour. This recording is carried out throughout the seven sessions which have been detailed earlier in Part III. Keeping diaries and a 'typical day' account is also useful.

Observation   In order to gauge directly the level of behavioural difficulties and the quality of parent-child interaction, a series of direct observation techniques are employed. These exercises focus particularly on the way instructions are given to children and the ability to reward and ignore behaviour. Typically, just over an hour is required to complete the observation.

Time sampling   This is a method of recording which enables data to be gathered for specific periods of the day. It is particularly useful if clients feel overwhelmed or if they are inconsistent in their record-keeping. An example of time sampling would be where tracking and recording showed that the highest frequency of a problem behaviour occurred at meal times. So therefore, a parent may wish to choose just dinnertime as the specific period for time sampling.

Graphs   These display the frequency of events or behaviour through simple line graphs. They visibly chart the level of progress from assessment stage through to intervention. Quite often parents 'feel' there is no improvement in their child's behaviour, so by seeing improvement represented in a simple graph, they feel more reassured and confident.

Cognition and emotional feelings   Cognitive behaviour therapy propounds the importance of measuring thought processes and their impact on the way a person feels and behaves. Understanding cognitive blocks can be important when dealing with parents who get stuck and feel unable to carry out practical tasks. Simple rating scales, such as 0–5 or 0–100, can be employed when monitoring the strength of specific thoughts. The scales can rate, for example, how bad a person feels, or the intensity of the situation.

Video and audio recording   The use of video and audio recording as 'fly on the wall' techniques can be extremely powerful for measuring patterns of interaction and communication. They can be helpful when working with people who have reading and writing difficulties. They can also be a very effective means of recording teenage communication.

11 Evaluating the Centre's results

Evaluating the fun and families groups

During the past four years the Centre for Fun and Families have continuously evaluated their work with both individual families and the groupwork programmes along lines outlined in Chapter 10. Below are a series of tables

Overall group evaluation

How well was the course organised and presented?	Range 3–5	Mean 4.12
How well were the practical elements explained and demonstrated	Range 3–5	Mean 4.12
Were the topics covered in sufficient depth?	Range 3–5	Mean 4.25
What level of progress do you feel you have made since the course started?	Range 2–5	Mean 3.50
What level of support and help did you receive from the other parents?	Range 2–5	Mean 4.00
Did the sessions demand too much or too little from you? Circle '0' if about right, a minus number if too little, a positive number if too much.	Range –1–0	Mean 4.00

Key: 0 = very poor, 1 = poor, 2 = fair, 3 = good, 4 = very good, 5 = excellent.

which give the results from evaluating the groups. (See Appendix C for evaluation chart, p. 144).

The box above shows an overall evaluation of a group run in 1989. The results are significantly high and typical of other groups run in a four-year period.

The above group convened in November 1989. The results are significantly high and are typical of other groups run throughout a four-year period. Nine questionnaires were completed and there was one dropout.

The list of comments below shows typical parental feedback at completion of a 7-week programme:

- 'Being a parent does not come naturally! The course helped me to understand what was going on and how I could change it.'
- 'I am now glad I stayed on the course as it helped tremendously, especially in nipping new behaviours in the bud prior to them becoming problems.'
- 'It was nice for a change that the social worker concentrated on helping me rather than just looking at the children.'
- 'Before attending the course I felt totally helpless and alone. Being able to share difficulties and get practical advice that works has helped me to be less confused and more confident about the future.'
- 'I can now see that my difficulties are not as unusual or as bad as I thought. This helps!'
- 'The course was great, but just when Pete's behaviour started to improve the group ended.'
- 'It helped me to become stronger when dealing with Kevin, but he seems to get stronger too.'
- 'A lot of people said to me that if I go on the course, the social worker will be solely looking at my past and whether I abuse my kids. By the time I went to the first meeting I was really uptight, even frightened. But now I know that they were talking rubbish. I feel proud of what I have achieved and that I cared enough to get help.'

There are many reasons why some parents have limited achievement on the groupwork programmes. Some have to do with the actual group itself:

- Poor attendance (though level of actual dropout is small)
- Size of the group, that is, above eight or below three
- Child-care problems, when wanting to attend the group.

Some group members have problems with their partners who may be:

- Unsupportive

- Working away from home
- Working shifts or long hours
- Having marital difficulties.

Some single-parent group members experience a lack of social support.

Group members cited problems with their children as reasons for limited progress:

- Long-standing child behaviour problems
- Confusion and lack of consistency in child management
- Long-standing patterns of negative parent-child interaction based on punishment and control.

Finally, some parents attain limited results from the group because of a lack of belief in positive change.

The above lists only represent 'potential' factors why parents do 'less well' on the programme. They should not be used to exclude individuals from attending because for many parents, the reason they join is because they are experiencing one or more of the above factors. Fun and families groups have been consistently shown to be effective over a wide client population, including families where there are acute child protection concerns. The large majority of parents do report a level of positive change. The essential therapeutic elements are listed below:

Logical structure

Step-by-step approach

Application of principles to individual circumstances

Full parental participation and involvement

Two group leaders

Power sharing re. strategies for change

Weekly recaps of each session

Constant reference to parental examples and own practice

Be clear and specific about 'target' or problem behaviour

Encourage social support between parents

Try to be imaginative and dynamic in your approach

If appropriate, offer individual advice

Empathy and rapport

Keeping on task

Practising of methods and techniques (within group and at home)

Humour and fun

Weekly 'homework' tasks

Evaluation by parents and group leaders

Keeping within time constraints (2 hrs. per session)

Relate behaviour to social learning theory

Negotiate measurable goals and objectives

Use exercises which reinforce 'team' working/building

Chase up parents who do not attend

The above points itemise what we have found to be essential requirements for running effective groupwork programmes. The table below shows the results from a groupwork programme. It provides evaluation results from the Eyeberg Child Behaviour Inventory, which measures the frequency of 37 behaviour difficulties and uses a 1–7 rating scale (never–always). A typical 'total frequency score' for a parent with child behaviour problems would be 160. The Eyeberg also asks whether each behaviour is currently seen as a problem or not. The results shown are from the same group used in the figure on p. 117. They demonstrate a significant reduction in the frequency of child behaviours and an average decline of over 50% in terms of numbers of problems (pre- and post-group). Comparatively, the results are similar to those of other groups that have been run during the last four years.

Evaluation results from the Eyeberg Child Behaviour Inventory

	Frequency score		Number of problems	
	Pre	Post	Pre	Post
Parent 1	167	86	21	7
Parent 2	166	117	16	4
Parent 3	154	83	19	0
Parent 4	187	143	24	17
Parent 5	152	129	19	14
Parent 6	164	136	16	6
Parent 7	117	113	12	3
Parent 8	188	137	27	18
Mean	162	118	19	9

Identifying parents' needs and feelings

We have encountered many negative parental thoughts and feelings in our fun and families groups. These include:

- Helplessness
- Powerlessness
- Loneliness
- 'What have I done to deserve this?'
- 'Nothing will ever change.'
- 'What do I do next?'
- 'I thought being a parent came naturally.'
- Frustration
- 'I smack because I don't know what else to do.'
- 'My child knows the right buttons to push to get me wound up.'

- Inadequacy
- Isolation
- 'Why me?'
- 'He is like a little devil.'
- 'It was never like this on TV.'
- 'My child hates me.'
- Resentment
- 'I feel like a coiled spring ready to explode.'
- 'Why are my friends' children like little angels?'
- 'I feel knackered and just a slave to my two year old.'

The list above is extremely relevant to practitioners engaged in family work as it identifies common parental needs which ought to be considered or addressed. Assessing experiences and stress factors which have generated negative thoughts and feelings is crucial, particularly in child protection work. Such ways of thinking and feeling can be highly destructive to family relationships as they mentally create a vicious circle. The child ultimately becomes the most vulnerable victim.

The statements in the list above were mainly gathered prior to the commencement of the groupwork programme.

Conclusion

The purpose of this chapter has been to promote a model of good practice and to demonstrate the usefulness of evaluation. It represents a set of principles and procedures which, if adhered to, facilitate planning, partnership and greater effectiveness. Such skills are vital when working within the principles of the Children Act.

Evaluation does not occur in a vacuum, as it represents a dynamic process clearly reflecting assessment and intervention. Future planning and the way a practitioner operates must also be informed by this process. We should not depend on our experience or professional instinct to tell us that our advice and intervention was right or effective, but we must instead generate clear evidence for our actions and results.

12 Parents' support groups

The need for parents' support groups

We have found that during the four years of running fun and families groups, the need for parents' support groups have become more and more noticeable and we have listed below what we believe are some of the reasons for this:

- Parents who have attended a fun and families group often feel quite bereft when the short seven-week course comes to an end. The support and friendship has become important to them. So, although few parents need further advice and support from us, many benefit from just getting out regularly, keeping company with other people who have common interests and taking some time for themselves away from the children.
- Some parents within the groups discover that some of their problems arise from conflicting advice about childhood development. They therefore develop a need to keep in touch with 'informed' opinion and informal support which helps them select what is right for them and encourages, rather than criticises or questions, their efforts.
- Many parents have friends who are too shy to attend the group programme. Gradually, they have been prepared to come to a less formal support group and consequently derive benefit from doing so. Some parents have even joined a fun and families group as a result of this.
- Research undertaken by Andy Gill shows that parents who did have support of an informal group maintained the progress they had achieved during the fun and family group far longer and more surely than those who did not.

How support groups have developed

At first, support groups were explored by putting people in touch with another parent living in the same area. This became a type of 'buddy' system, but it had only limited success. We have found, through experience, and trial and error, that support groups really take off when parents themselves take matters into their own hands and do not depend on the groupwork facilitators to set it up. The original intention was to set the seventh session of the groupwork programme one month after the main agenda was finished. The idea here was to offer a chance to see how people were doing and to provide a booster or extra help if parents wanted this. The parents returned after the month and had obviously missed the group members and the weekly sessions. From this, parents began to think about forming their own support groups.

In rural Leicestershire, for example, meetings began in the parents' own homes. They began to invite speakers as well as using the meetings for purely social events. This meant that the topics and activities varied and were really what they wanted for themselves. In Bradford, a support group formed a lobby and got a petition together to the Housing Committee to improve the lot of those struggling in temporary accommodation. They themselves were sure that little more could be done to help themselves and their children until their living conditions and housing needs were addressed. A Melton Mowbray group in Leicestershire arranged a programme of assertiveness training as a follow-on from a fun and families group. In the Wirral a 'Feeling Good' programme was set up. This was to help parents enjoy themselves and appreciate their own strengths and qualities. There has since been a follow-on course called 'Stay Feeling Good'.

Some practical points we have learned

Although the meetings held in individual homes flourished, it also became clear that some structure would be needed to help the group survive and gain the most advantage from their endeavours. Keeping in touch with each other and organising speakers all involved time and cost such as telephone calls and postage. Therefore, small committees were formed and they acquired small amounts of funding from local charities and Social Services community grants. Group leaders continued to offer encouragement, but parents designed and organised their own programmes. In one group, 40 people were involved and meetings attracted 8–20 participants.

Some parents began to publicise their group in the local free press and included a telephone number as a contact point. Funds were raised and stationary was printed. There also began to be a forum where new ideas and suggestions for improvement of the fun and families programme was generated. One example of this was the suggestion by parents that we should give certificates to parents who had completed the seven-week course.

The main practical issues revolve around:

- Finding a warm comfortable room to meet in
- Organising tea and coffee facilities
- Organising a crèche or child-minding scheme
- Someone to be the secretary who will pull the group together and remind people what is happening each week
- Someone to act as treasurer if funding and fundraising is to be an issue
- Organising social activities if this is wanted
- Providing some programme or focus for meetings.

Some ideas for well-received topics

The range and extent of well-received topics has been wide. Some of these have been: diet and behaviour, anxious children, sleep problems and night terrors, defiance and tantrums, toilet-training, child development, children's health, communicating with children, preparing for school, speech difficulties and coping with aggression. One session that went down very well was 'Children Playing'. This was an hilarious evening in which parents recaptured their own childhood, playing games which they had long since abandoned or forgotten about!

Whenever possible local speakers were invited, such as nurses, teachers, doctors and health visitors. Generally, they enjoyed the opportunity to relate in a less formal way to a group of parents.

The kind of social activities that have gone down well have been: beer and skittles, children's parties, parents' fun night and family outings.

Some lessons we have learned from parents

We have learned that trying to suggest or help set up support groups ourselves does not work very well. The initiative needs to come from the parents themselves. The more effort the groupwork leaders put into setting them up, the more it seems that the parents feel the support group is almost a continuation of the fun and families course. They therefore come to rely on the leaders for ideas, suggestions, organisation and initiative. The parents feel more empowered and in control if the initiative comes from them. We have therefore strongly advocated this. A group in Hinckley found that by about the fifth session of the programme, parents began automatically to think about what would happen after the seven weeks were finished. From this, a support group began to be thought about, so that by the end of the seven weeks they had already planned and organised their group. This was fully organised and run by themselves. They then went on to form a women's group as a result of this process.

Several fun and families groups have been run within the Asian community in Leicester. However, support groups have not so far materialised. Some Asian people from different professional groups have felt that the fun and families programme does not yet have a strong enough identification in the local community and that more time is needed for this to happen. However, the last groupwork programme in 1995 attracted over 20 parents, even without advertising. Parents seemed to come purely by 'word of mouth'. So, we are still optimistic that support groups will happen!

Support groups generally have been completely open. Anyone can join or leave as they choose. This has useful spin-offs, as some people then pluck up enough courage to join a fun and families group. A downside to such flexibility is that the burden of keeping the group going falls on a few willing shoulders. This inevitably means that such people move on to new interests and there have to be people willing to take over. Generally, this is the case with various types of groups where their life is limited and unpredictable. However, this does not really matter for new people do emerge and start their own particular style of group in due course.

The achievements of support groups

Parents involved in these groups gained considerable confidence. Some of them shared in presenting workshops at the inaugural conference of the Centre for Fun and Families. Others took part in and helped to produce a video on child behaviour entitled *Positive Ways of Coping with Children's Behaviour*. This video is available from the Centre for training and discussion work.

Parents from a very varied range of backgrounds have shared in the activities mentioned in this chapter. They have come from different social classes and ethnic groups, and have experienced varying degrees of difficulty with their children. Some very severe behaviour problems, including some that have been made more acute by worrying medical conditions, have been addressed. Other parents have had mental health problems themselves. Some parents have come just because they want more information. There have also been those parents who felt defeated and in need of reassurance. Generally speaking, they have found it from others in the group.

The sharing and giving to each other has been an exhilarating and reciprocal experience. One parent observed, 'If a head teacher [who was in the group] can have problems, it cannot be so bad that I find it tough.' Another highly competent parent came to realise her own high expectations and standards were most unusual and were making a rod for her own back.

These lessons were learned without instruction. They happened by merely being together and sharing a sense of belonging. Meeting together has created loyalties and incentives. Many parents acknowledge they may have felt like giving up, but did not want to let their friends down or to lose face. Quite often, even when some parents already knew what to do to resolve their children's difficult behaviours, they became aware that 'going it alone' can erode resolve.

The rediscovery of energy has been amazing. People struggling with their own finances suddenly wanted to help raise money for the group, or other groups. Parents who felt they were now managing quite well, found time to visit someone else who just needed guidance and a little support and company.

Generally, within the support groups, unexpected potential and enthusiasm has emerged and personal strength and growth has blossomed in a most moving way. After four years of running fun and families groups, we now feel that support groups are now a vital and natural complement to our groupwork programmes. We wholeheartedly welcome this development.

Part V

The Centre and you: resources and future developments

13 How can we help you?

This book was written as a practical sourcebook so that anyone in the caring professions could use it as a comprehensive 'how to do it' guide for running a fun and families group. We try to provide a clear theoretical background for those workers who have either never been involved in groupwork or used social learning theory before. We have also provided a very detailed description of the groupwork programme. In addition, we intended to make it useful for those workers who have already had some experience of running groups by providing summaries and checklists to assist in the planning process.

However, no one book can be sufficient for everyone's purposes and we would be sad to feel that, having used the book and run a group, workers should not feel enthusiastic and confident enough to go further and make use of other sources and references. Furthermore, Tom Douglas (1991) reminds us that in groupwork 'the transfer of knowledge into practice is best performed in an apprenticeship system or in well supervised practice' (p. 144).

With this in mind the Centre has provided a range of resources for workers to use either in the planning, running or evaluation of their work in running fun and families groupwork programmes.

Resources from the Centre

Workshops

The Centre is able to offer workshops for 12–20 people that can be run in your own agency.

The workshop 'Setting up and running a fun and families group' is designed to offer training on all aspects of the planning and running of a fun and families group. The training also offers a pack of hand-outs and resources that allow workers to run a group. The trainers have copies of all the booklets, video- and audio-tape material, plus fun stickers and albums that the Centre produces available for those who want them. Workers who have attended the training are also able to have access to our free post-training consultancy service.

Consultancy service

This service is most useful where there is a very small group of staff, from 2–6 people, who already have some experience of groupwork or social learning theory who want to spend some time, usually 3–4 hours, with one of the Centre staff discussing their plans to run a fun and families group. Again the Centre's resources will be available, whether the consultancy is undertaken in your agency or at the Centre.

Call back days

Where staff have either attended Centre workshops or consultancies and have been able to run a fun and families group, a call back day can be helpful. The day can be used to review the workers' experience of running a group and look at ways of building on the successful aspects and avoiding the difficulties that were encountered. The agenda for these days can be in the hands of those attending. A programme can be devised by the potential participants completing a brief questionnaire about their experiences of running a group. The Centre staff can then devise a programme that addresses the common themes identified from the participants' responses. The Centre staff find these days very exciting to run because the enthusiasm and confidence of the workers at the end of these call back days is infectious!

Booklets, video- and audio-tape, and fun stickers and albums

The collection of resources available, price list and order form are available in our resources catalogue. This is available free from the Centre and is updated once or twice a year. We also have a range of hand-outs, charts, articles and questionnaires that are useful in specific circumstances such as in working with children with disabilities, teenagers or focusing on specific behaviours such as bed-wetting. You are welcome to ring and enquire if any item you want is not in the resources catalogue.

Combined membership and 200 Club

You can become a member of the Centre. This entitles you to attend the Annual General Meeting and receive priority copies of the Centre's newsletter. In addition, you automatically are entered into the 200 Club which is drawn monthly, plus an extra Christmas draw. You will also have the satisfaction of supporting the further development of the work of the Centre.

Our hope is that you will make use of the services of the Centre. We are very keen to know that we have not written a 'dead' book. By this we mean that in writing the book we have intended to communicate a set of ideas about practice based upon our experience. We hope that in doing so you will also feel encouraged to use those ideas that are helpful, but also to communicate with us if you feel any of the ideas are unhelpful or unclear. Most of all we would also be delighted to hear of your successes and for you to share with us where you feel practice to the benefit of parents and children can be improved. Our long-term aim would be to create a network of national and regional support groups for people who are running fun and families groups so that this process of sharing can take place. However, until that hope becomes reality we will look forward to hearing from you direct!

14 Future developments

In Chapter 1, we listed the achievements of the Centre since its formation as a national voluntary organisation in June 1990. It is worthwhile to summarise these briefly as a preamble to looking at ways we feel the Centre can most usefully develop in the future.

The Centre's achievements

1 The Centre has established itself as a national voluntary organisation with charitable status. It has a range of contacts throughout the country, produces regular newsletters and has begun to develop a regional consultancy system.
2 The Centre has an active governing body and fundraising sub-committee and produces a range of information about its activities through its workshop programme, resources catalogue, student placements booklet and several information booklets for parents.
3 The Centre runs groups for parents, in partnership with other agencies, in almost all parts of Leicestershire and has also been developing the 'Living with Teenagers' programme.
4 The Centre has developed a core of six workshops that it runs for statutory and voluntary agencies throughout the country. In addition the Centre also offers a consultancy service.
5 The Centre produces a range of resources, including nine booklets, one video, a relaxation tape and fun stickers and albums.
6 The Centre has produced an anti-discriminatory practice policy and Action Plan and has undertaken groupwork with Asian parents. The translation of information and group hand-outs into other languages has been developed.

135

7   The Centre now offers six placements per year for students on MA/ Diploma in Social Work courses.

Future possibilities

The last four years have demonstrated to the Centre that:

- There is a consistently high demand for the training/consultancy and student placement services that the Centre provides.
- The demand from parents to attend group programmes continues to be very high and the demands from the parents of teenagers shows every indication of being equally as high.
- The continued growth in demand in both areas indicates that the Centre is meeting needs that are *not* met by any other statutory or voluntary agency.

Within the Centre itself our plans are not limited by a shortage of ideas about what we hope to achieve in the future. The main limitation is a shortage of money to take the ideas further and to make them a reality. From discussions we have had, the staff see the following key developments as being on our agenda for the next two to three years.

Living with Teenagers' programme

This programme uses the same theoretical foundation as the fun and families programme but focuses more on skills of listening, communication, problem-solving, negotiating and the use of agreements. It has only been run twice and would benefit from further refinement and improvement. We can also see the need for some expansion and variation of some of the video- and audio-tape material. There is also a need to experiment with some sessions where the teenagers attend themselves, rather than just the parents.

National link person system

We feel that it is important to offer more support to workers from statutory and voluntary agencies who are running fun and families groups throughout the country. This system would allow good practice and new ideas about the programme to be shared nationwide.

Parent's manual

At present group leaders are only able to provide parents with a folder to store papers hand-outs or record charts during and after the group. We would like to develop a 'ring binder' type of manual. This would allow papers and charts to be kept safely and in logical order and sequence. It would also give the material a more professional appearance. However, we want to avoid a glossy printed manual. This is mainly because the moment it is printed it will become out of date and inflexible. In addition, the glossy manual gives the impression of being a 'teaching aid' or 'expert's manual' which is a concept the group programme is attempting to avoid.

Anti-discriminatory practice

Within our Action Plan we intend to expand in the following areas. First, we would wish to achieve the translation of a much greater percentage of our material into other languages. Second, we would like to run groups for parents of African/Caribbean origin to test the programme's applicability within these communities; this is planned for May 1995. Third, we would like to develop the fun and families programme to make it more relevant to parents of children with disabilities. Finally, we would like to make links with organisations that represent gay people to attempt to discover their preferences in terms of the groupwork services the Centre can offer to gay parents. In the longer term we would like to employ a black member of staff, subject to money being available for this purpose.

Parental involvement

The Centre has attempted to involve parents who have attended groups in a variety of ways. First, we have promoted the running of their own parents' support groups after the groupwork programme finishes. Second, we have asked parents to attend the first session of new groups to motivate new parents and to tell the participants how they benefited from the group. Third, we have attempted to persuade parents to join the Centre's Governing Body and to become involved in the Centre's fundraising activities. Finally, parents are encouraged to use their talents and skills to promote the work of the Centre. For example, one parent who was a yoga teacher did a part-session on relaxation. Another parent with artistic skills designed and produced the Centre's fun stickers and albums.

However, we feel that some parents could play a part in running a fun and families group and also assist us in the training. We feel this is an aim we would like to achieve, despite the fact that there are many practical obstacles.

Permanent funding

The Centre currently receives no regular funding from any statutory body. While receiving funding is not an end in itself, but a means to achieving the aims set out above, it is an important objective for the Centre to acquire some reasonably secure, stable and regular form of funding. This would be useful because it would encourage the Centre to plan in a more systematic and long-term way. Unstable funding tends to produce more of a crisis management approach which does not lead to the best use of the Centre's staff resources. Consequently, the aims set out above are much more likely to be achieved if a substantial and stable source of funding is found.

Concluding remarks

In this chapter on future developments we have, hopefully, given you an insight into aspects of our work that are likely to be successfully developed over the next few years. In addition, we hope we have raised your enthusiasm for running fun and families groups for parents to the point that you want to do more than read about it and to start thinking about when you are going to run your first group. Or, if you have already run one, to start planning your next one. The other equally important message we hope to have conveyed, is that you are not alone. If you run into difficulties or would like to talk to someone else who has run a group, you are welcome to contact the Centre and we will either try to answer your query or put you in touch with someone locally in your region who you can talk to.

We would like to conclude by offering the observation that in the last decade child protection and crisis interventions into the lives of families have been too predominant as a form of professional intervention. Sadly, this style of work has proved both unsuccessful, highly unpopular with families and extremely negative for the professional staff who have to undertake such work. In offering a model of work that shows family support can be economical, efficient and effective – and also fun – we hope we have made some contribution to turning the tide towards a more positive image for the caring professions.

Appendices

Appendix A: Recording form

Name ....

Date chart commenced ....

In the event of any problems developing please

contact ....

Tel. No ....

	7–8	8–9	9–10	10–11	11–12	12–1	1–2	2–3	3–4	4–5	5–6	6–7	7–8	8–9	9–10	10–4	4–7
Mon																	
Tues																	
Wed																	
Thurs																	
Fri																	
Sat																	
Sun																	

Please record the target behaviour on the above chart *each time* it occurs.

Target BAD behaviour A is defined as:

Target GOOD behaviour B is defined as:

141

Appendix B: Evaluation form (child's behaviour)

Below are a series of phrases that describe children's behaviour. First, could you please circle the number which accurately describes *how often* the behaviour currently occurs with your child. Second, circle *yes* or *no* to indicate whether the behaviour is *a problem for you*.

		Never	*Seldom*	*Sometimes*	*Often*	*Always*	*Is this a problem?*	
1	Continually demands things	1	2	3	4	5	yes	no
2	Is defiant when asked to do something	1	2	3	4	5	yes	no
3	Is slow or lingers at mealtimes	1	2	3	4	5	yes	no
4	Refuses to go to bed on time	1	2	3	4	5	yes	no
5	Won't sleep in his/her bed	1	2	3	4	5	yes	no
6	Has temper tantrums	1	2	3	4	5	yes	no
7	Whines	1	2	3	4	5	yes	no
8	Is aggressive towards parents	1	2	3	4	5	yes	no
9	Fights with brothers and sisters	1	2	3	4	5	yes	no
10	Enjoys 'winding up' parents	1	2	3	4	5	yes	no
11	Interrupts	1	2	3	4	5	yes	no
12	Has short attention span	1	2	3	4	5	yes	no
13	Continually wakes up at night	1	2	3	4	5	yes	no
14	Has bad dreams or 'night terrors'	1	2	3	4	5	yes	no
15	Is aggressive towards friends or playmates	1	2	3	4	5	yes	no

Other behaviour difficulties not listed or not accurately described above:

		Never	Seldom	Sometimes	Often	Always	Is this a problem?	
16	....	1	2	3	4	5	yes	no
17	....	1	2	3	4	5	yes	no
18	....	1	2	3	4	5	yes	no
19	....	1	2	3	4	5	yes	no

Finally, can you identify specific good behaviours, however small, and circle the correct number which best indicates how frequently they occur.

		Sometimes	Often	Always
1	....	1	2	3
2	....	1	2	3
3	....	1	2	3
4	....	1	2	3

Thank you for completing this questionnaire. The information will enable you to contrast the situation at the end of the course when it is hoped that your child's behaviour will have significantly improved.

Name ....   Date ....

Appendix C: Parents' evaluation of groupwork

Please rate the course by circling a number on each of the scales below. Add any comments which you might want to make.

0 = very poor, 1 = poor, 2 = fair, 3 = good, 4 = very good, 5 = excellent

1   How well were the sessions organised
    and presented?   0   1   2   3   4   5

2   How well were the practical issues
    explained?   0   1   2   3   4   5

3   Were topics covered in sufficient
    depth?   0   1   2   3   4   5

4   Did the sessions demand too much or
    too little from you? Circle 0 if about
    right, a minus number if too little,
    or a positive number if too much.   −2   −1   0   1   2

5   Suggestions for future courses, for example changes in content or emphasis:

6   General comments on how the course has/has not helped you in handling your child's behaviour problems.

Thank you for completing this questionnaire! Your comments will be used.

References

Ahmad, B. (1990) *Black Perspectives in Social Work*. Birmingham: Ventura Press.

Bandura, A. (1971) *Social Learning Theory*. Morristown, New Jersey: General Learning Press.

Beck, A.T. (1976) *Cognitive Therapy and the Emotional Disorders*. New York: New American Library.

Beck, A.T. *et al.* (1990) *Cognitive Therapy of Personality Disorders*. New York: Guildford Press.

Beresford, P. and Croft, S. (1990) *From Paternalism to Participation*. London: Open Services Project.

Davis, L. and Proctor, E. (1989) *Race, Gender and Class: Guidelines for Practice with Individuals, Families and Groups*. London: Prentice-Hall.

Dominelli, L. (1988) *Anti-Racist Social Work*. London: Macmillan.

Douglas, T. (1991) *A Handbook of Common Groupwork Problems*. London: Routledge.

Dryden, W. and Golden, W. (1986) *Cognitive Approaches to Psychotherapy*. London: Harper and Row.

Dryden, W. and Scot, M. (1990) *An Introduction to Cognitive-Behaviour Therapy: Theory and Applications*. Liverpool: Liverpool Personal Services Society.

Ellis, A. (1973) *Humanistic Psychotherapy: The Rational Emotive Approach*. New York: The Julian Press.

Eyeberg, S. *et al.* (1980) 'Inventory of Child Problem Behaviours', *Journal of Clinical Child Psychology*, Spring, pp. 22–9.

Falloon, I. *et al.* (1984) *Family Care of Schizophrenia*. New York: Guildford Press.

Gambrill, E.D. (1977) *Behaviour Modification Handbook of Assessment, Intervention and Evaluation*. San Francisco and London: Jossey Bass.

Gill, A. (1989a) *Groupwork Programme Evaluation Questionnaire*. Leicester: Centre for Fun and Families.

Gill, A. (1989b) 'Putting Fun Back into Families', *Social Work Today*, 4 May, pp. 14–15.

Gill, A. (1989c) *Questionnaire to Measure Parental Attitudes, Attributions and Emotional Feelings*. Leicester: Centre for Fun and Families.

Gill, A. (1989d) *Structured Observation of Parent–Child Interaction*. Leicester: Centre for Fun and Families.

Hawton, K. *et al.* (1990) *Cognitive Behaviour Therapy for Psychiatric Problems: A Practical Guide*. Oxford University Press.

Herbert, M. (1987) *Behavioural Treatment of Children with Problems*. London: Academic Press.

Herbert, M. (1988) *Working with Children and their Families*. London: Routledge.

Herbert, M. (1991) *Child Care and the Family: A Client Management Resource Pack*. Windsor: NFER-Nelson Ltd.

Lazarus, A. (1971) *Behaviour Therapy and Beyond*. New York: McGraw-Hill.

MacDonald, I. (1991) *All Equal Under the Act?* London: Race Equality Unit, National Institute for Social Work.

McMullin, R. and Giles, T. (1981) *Cognitive Behaviour Therapy – Restructuring Approach*. New York: Gruve & Stretton.

Martin, P. and Bateson, P. (1986) *Measuring Behaviour*. Cambridge: Cambridge University Press.

Meichenbaum, D. (1985) *Stress Inoculation Training*. New York: Pergamon.

Meichenbaum, D. (1987) *Cognitive Behaviour Modification*. New York: Plenum.

Paterson, G.R. (1974) 'Retraining of Aggressive Boys by their Parents: Review of Recent Literature and Follow-up Evaluation', *Journal of the Canadian Psychiatric Association*, Vol. 19, No. 2, pp. 142–57.

Paterson, G.R. (1994) 'War and Peace', *Community Care*, 4 April.

Preston-Shoot, M. (1987) *Effective Groupwork*. London: BASW Publications, Macmillan Education Ltd.

Schuyler, D. (1991) *A Practical Guide to Cognitive Therapy*. New York and London: Norton and Company.

Sheldon, B. (1982) *Behaviour Modification: Theory, Practice and Philosophy*. London: Tavistock.

Thompson, N. (1993) *Anti-Discriminatory Practice*. London: Macmillan.

Walen, S. *et al.* (1980) *A Practitioner's Guide to Rational Emotive Therapy*. New York: Oxford University Press.